New CLAIT

Unit 1

Using a Computer

The Course Book

CGP's Course Books offer a step-by-step approach to help you really get to grips with New CLAIT.

Each topic is explained using everyday language, with plenty of worked examples, handy hints and practical tasks.

Exactly what you need — perfect for even the most 'computer-phobic' learners.

Contents

Section One — Introduction

Section Two — Using a Computer

Section Three — Entering Text

Section Four — Opening, Closing, Saving and Printing

Section Five — The Assessment

Published by Coordination Group Publications Ltd.

Contributors:
Jo Anson
Charley Darbishire
Dominic Hall
Simon Little
Kate Manson
Rachel Selway
Jennifer Underwood

Endorsed by OCR for use with OCR Level 1 Certificate for IT users - New CLAIT specification

With thanks to Jackie Sherman for the proof-reading.
Thanks also to Robert Edwards and Julie Forsdick for their reviews throughout the project.

ISBN 1 84146 324 8

Groovy website: www.cgpbooks.co.uk
Jolly bits of clipart from CorelDRAW
Printed by Elanders Hindson, Newcastle upon Tyne.

With thanks to Microsoft for permission to use screenshots from
MS Word XP and MS Windows XP.

What is New CLAIT?

Here's a page to let you know what this book is all about.

New CLAIT is a Computer Course for Beginners

In New CLAIT, you'll learn how to make computers work for you, so you can use things like:

- word processors — to write letters
- spreadsheets — to do your household accounts
- databases — to organise information
- email — to keep in touch with people all over the world

Just Have a Go, You Won't Break it

The key to learning about computers is to try things.
Don't be afraid of it — you won't break the computer with a mouse and keyboard.
You'd need to open it up and pour a cup of tea inside to break it.

This book will take you through everything step-by-step. You'll be doing things all the time.

When you've got to do things, you'll find numbered shapes like this.

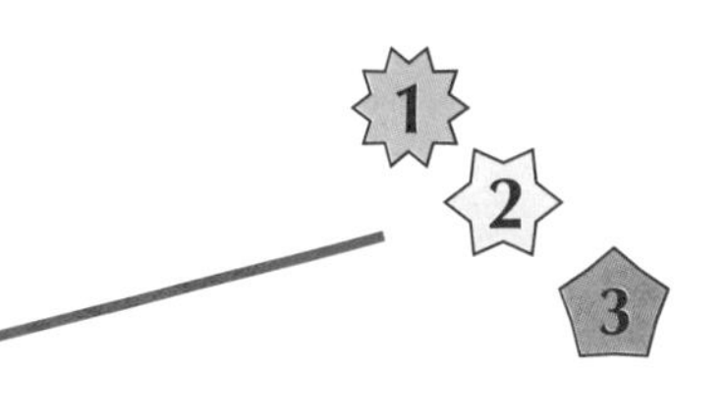

There are also practice exercises at the end of each section, so you can see how you'd do in a real New CLAIT test.

Read this bit if you are a Tutor

1) We've used Office XP and Windows XP Professional for this book, but most things will be the same for older versions.

2) To keep things simple we've concentrated on one way of doing things instead of confusing people with five different ways to do the same thing.

3) There is a CD which accompanies this series of books. It contains all the files the student will need for the worked examples, practice exercises and exams. It also contains sample answer files for most of the exercises. The files have been saved in Word 95 format for maximum compatibility. In the OCR assessment they'll be in .txt format.

Relax — computers are friendly...

This book tells you everything you need to pass New CLAIT Unit 1.
So just relax, have a go and enjoy it — you won't break your computer by just having a go.

The Bits of a Computer

This is a nice straightforward page to ease you into the course. You don't even have to switch your computer on yet — just have a look at it and learn what each bit does.

The Parts of a Computer Do Different Jobs

Here's a computer — and all the bits are labelled.

Monitor — looks like a TV screen. What you're working on is displayed on it.

System box — the 'brain' of the computer, where all the bits and pieces that make it work can be found. You put CDs and disks in here, and plug all the other computer parts into the back.

Printer — used to make a paper copy of what's on your screen, like letters or photos.

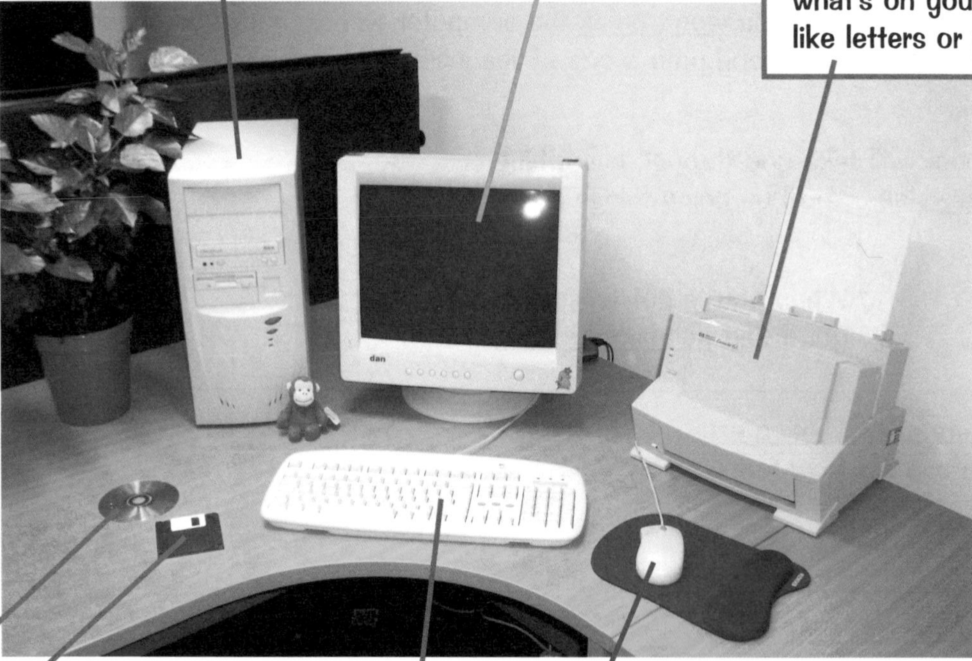

CDs and floppy disks — can be used to store your work. You can put them into a different computer and your work will appear.

Mouse — when you move this over your desk, a little arrow on the screen will move too. You can use it to select and change different things on the screen.

Keyboard — has keys with letters and numbers on that you press to enter information, e.g. to write a letter.

Ah, so that's what that thing in the spare room is...

So now you know about computers — at least you can tell them apart from, say, a toaster. Still a bit of work to go before you can apply for a job at NASA, but you're on the way.

The Bits of a Computer

You know what the different bits of a computer are called, but there's a bit more to learn yet...

Computers come in Different Shapes

Laptops are handy little computers that you can fold up, carry about in a bag and use on the train, should you fancy. They're as good as normal computers, just smaller.

Notebooks are like laptops, but smaller and a bit less powerful. (Still plenty good enough for us normal folks though.)

Computers are made of Hardware and Software

HARDWARE is all the physical bits of a computer — not just the obvious bits like the monitor, keyboard and printer, but also the gubbins inside that make it work.

SOFTWARE is all the programs in a computer that make it do different things — i.e. the instructions that tell the computer what to do. You can buy new software on CDs.

For example, Microsoft Word is a program which lets you write letters and things. A computer game is another program, where the keys you press might guide a character round a special world. Nice.

Here are Some Terms You'll Need to Know

1) Programs, like Word or Excel, are called applications.
2) Files are made with applications. They contain the things you make — a file from a word processor, like Word, will be lots of text, and a file from a drawing program will be a picture.
3) A folder is a place where you can store files or applications. They're really useful for organising your computer.

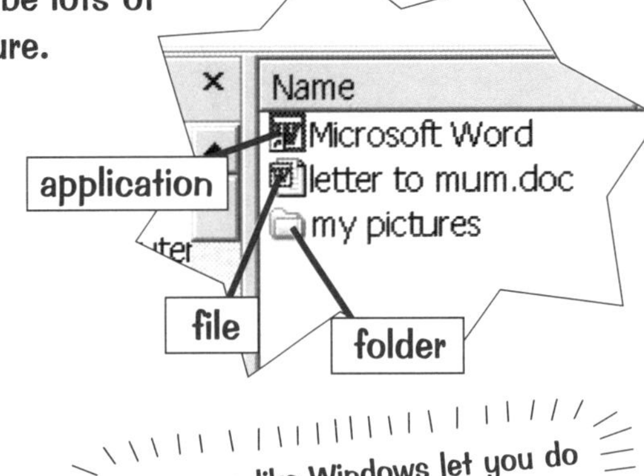

Windows is a special program called an 'operating system' — it lets you interact with the computer, open and close other programs, and generally control what's going on — useful.

Programs like Windows let you do loads of things without having to understand what's really going on.

Don't worry about the technical stuff...

It's good to try and understand how computers work, but it's more important to learn how to use them properly. So long as you can make them work for you, you're doing it right.

Using the Keyboard

Ah, the keyboard. The bit that looks like a typewriter. As easy to use as pressing buttons.

All Keyboards Look the Same (More or Less)

The big bit with the letters on is always the same — it's the same arrangement as on a typewriter. So if you've used a typewriter before, you should pick it up really easily.

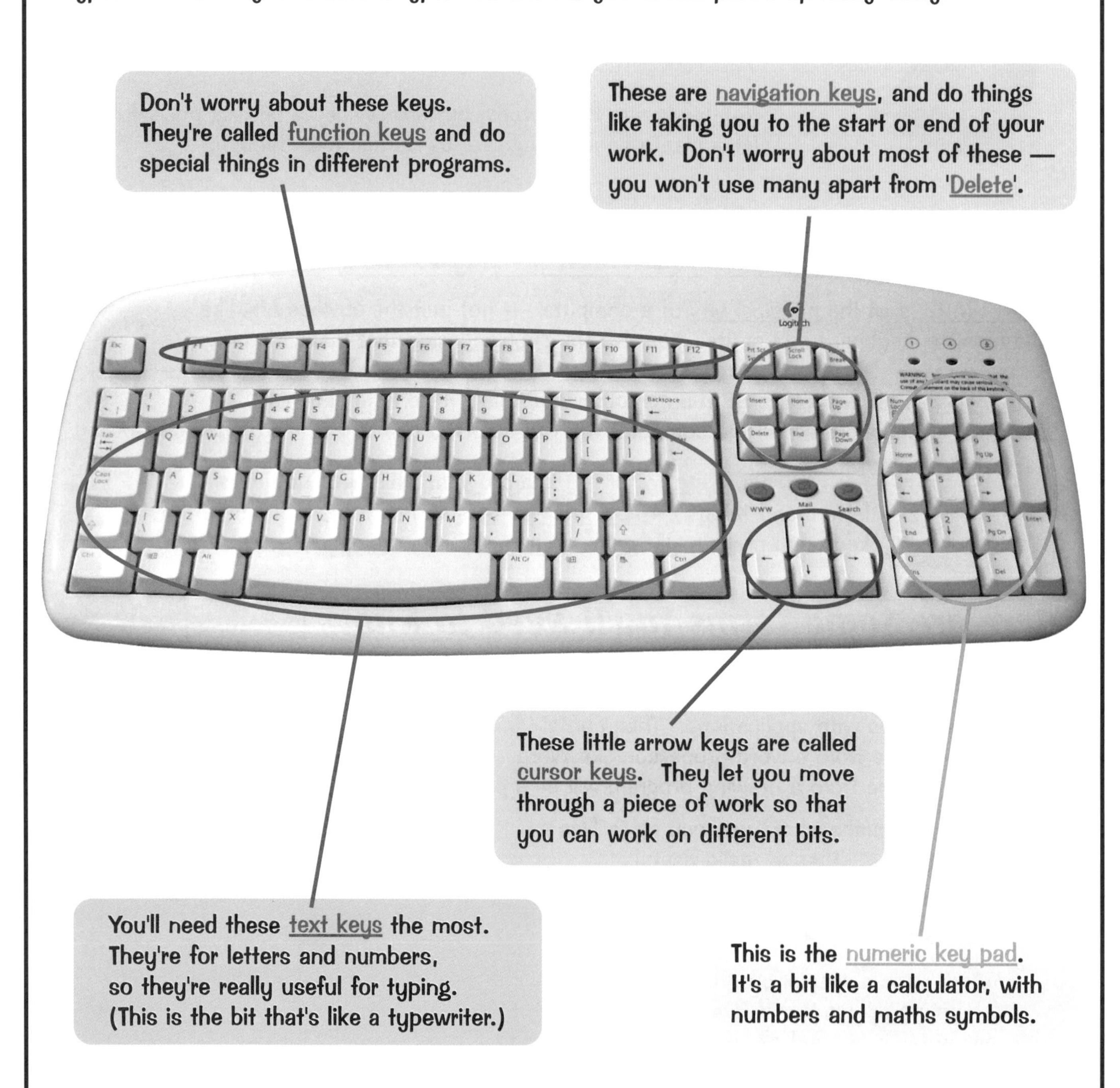

Keyboard — it's a board with keys on it...

Hard to believe, but you'll only need to use about 50% of your keyboard. Apparently we only use about 20% of our brains though, so we should be used to this kind of wastage by now.

Using the Keyboard

And now you know which bits to ignore, here's how to use some of the other bits.

Some Keys are Really Special

Here's some of the keys you'll find really useful when you're typing:

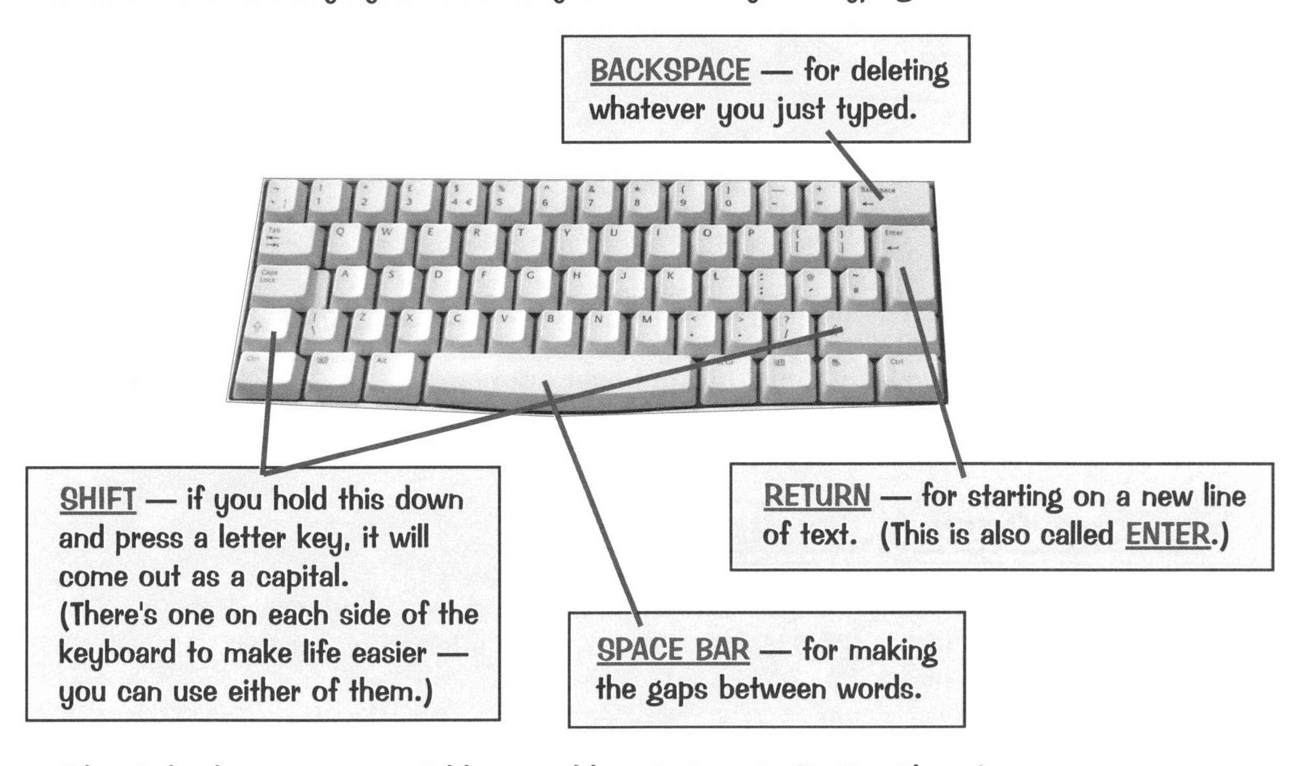

(There's loads more on special keys and how to type in Section Three.)

Have a Go at Using the Keyboard

Learning to type is really slow to begin with, but you'll soon get better with practice.
So, get someone to switch your computer on and open up Word or Notepad.
(Don't worry about learning to do this just yet — we'll be coming to it later.)

Then have a go at typing:

- You'll want to use one hand (or even one finger), but try to have a go with both.
- You don't have to whack the keys — find out how lightly you can press a key to still make it work.
- Have a play with the four special keys above.

The key to success — learn your keys...

Learning how to use a keyboard isn't hard. It's all those extra keys you don't need that make it look scary. Just press the letter and number keys and see what happens...

Get Used to the Mouse

The mouse — a cute, furry, cheese-loving mammal? Not this time. This mouse isn't a cheese fan.

First, Catch Your Mouse...

This is a mouse.

This is its right button (which you won't need for now).

This is its left button.

This is a mouse mat.

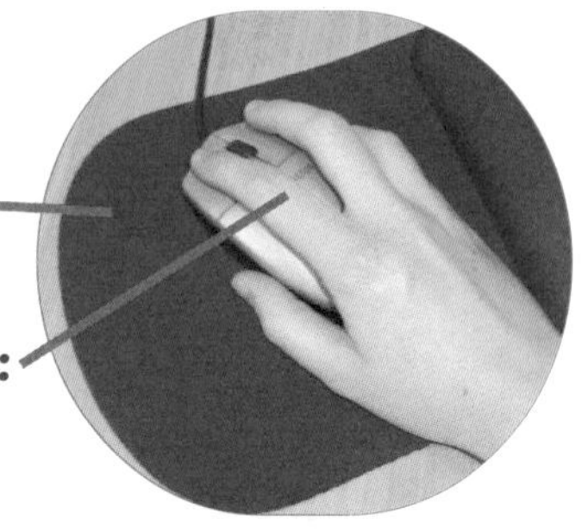

The mouse has a nice rounded top that you put your palm on, and a couple of buttons at the top where your fingers go. Like this:

...Then Push it Around a bit

1) To use your mouse, all you have to do is push it around on your desk. (You'll find that it glides along nicely on top of a foamy mouse mat.)

2) Underneath the mouse will be a little ball or a little red light. This bit tells the computer how you are moving the mouse.

3) As you move the mouse, a little arrow on your screen moves about. This arrow is called a pointer.

Pointers look a bit like this. (But they're about ten times tinier.)

When you're using writing software, like Word, your pointer will look like this, but a lot smaller.

Don't worry if your pointer looks different to the ones above. It'll be really obvious — the pointer is the thing that moves about on your screen when you move the mouse.

Just don't try to feed it cheese...

The best advice on learning to use a mouse is to just give it a go. Push it around and practise landing the pointer in certain places on the screen. It'll be weird at first, but you'll soon get it.

Get Used to the Mouse

And now, following on from how to spot a mouse, how to use it properly.

You'll need to use the Left Mouse Button all the time

You normally just 'click' the mouse button — give it a quick press and then take your finger off again — you'll hear a little clicking noise.

- The left mouse button can 'select' things. This means that when you move the pointer over something and click your left mouse button, you'll make it 'alive' and useable.
- If you 'double-click' the left mouse button — quickly click on something twice — you'll be able to open programs and make things work.

Try this Quick Activity for Learning Mouse Control

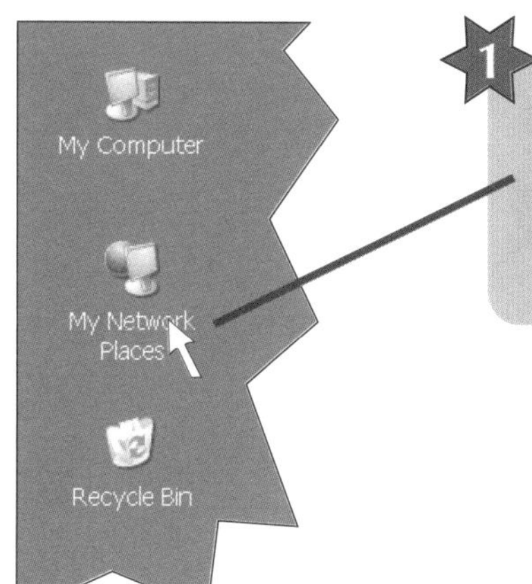

1. Move the mouse around until the pointer on the screen is on top of an icon. (An icon is a little picture, representing a file or application.)

See page 14 for more about icons and stuff.

2. Click the left mouse button once. The icon will get darker — become highlighted. This means you have selected it.

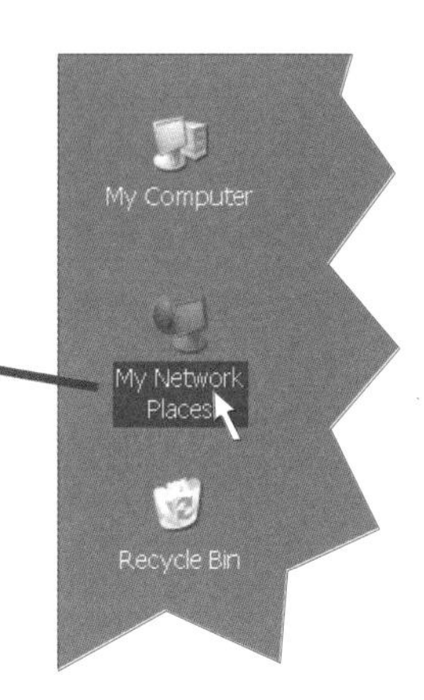

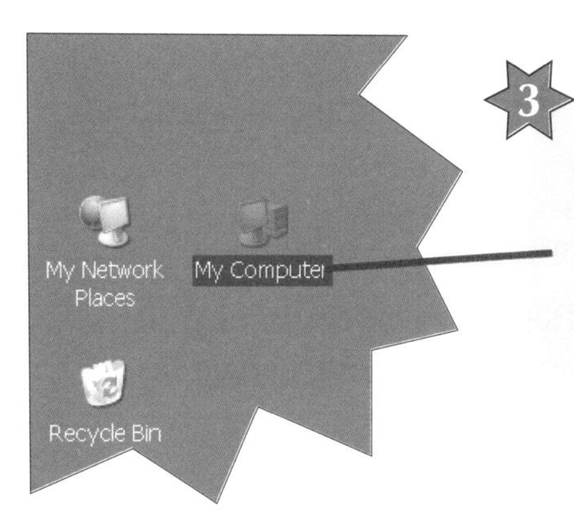

3. Move the pointer over a different icon. Press the left mouse button down and keep it held down. Then move your mouse and you'll find you can drag the icon about. Useful.

4. If you 'double-click' on an icon (move your pointer to it and do a quick 'click click'), you'll make it open.

Click click, fun fun fun...

This does sound a bit confusing on paper, but once you've had a go at the clicking, you'll be fine. What you've got to remember is — left once selects, left twice opens, left-hold-move drags.

Computer Health and Safety

Bet you thought you knew how to sit already. Well, now you're going to learn properly.

You Should Learn to Sit Properly at a Computer

Here's a half-naked muscle-man — let's call him Brian.
Brian's going to show how you should sit at a computer.

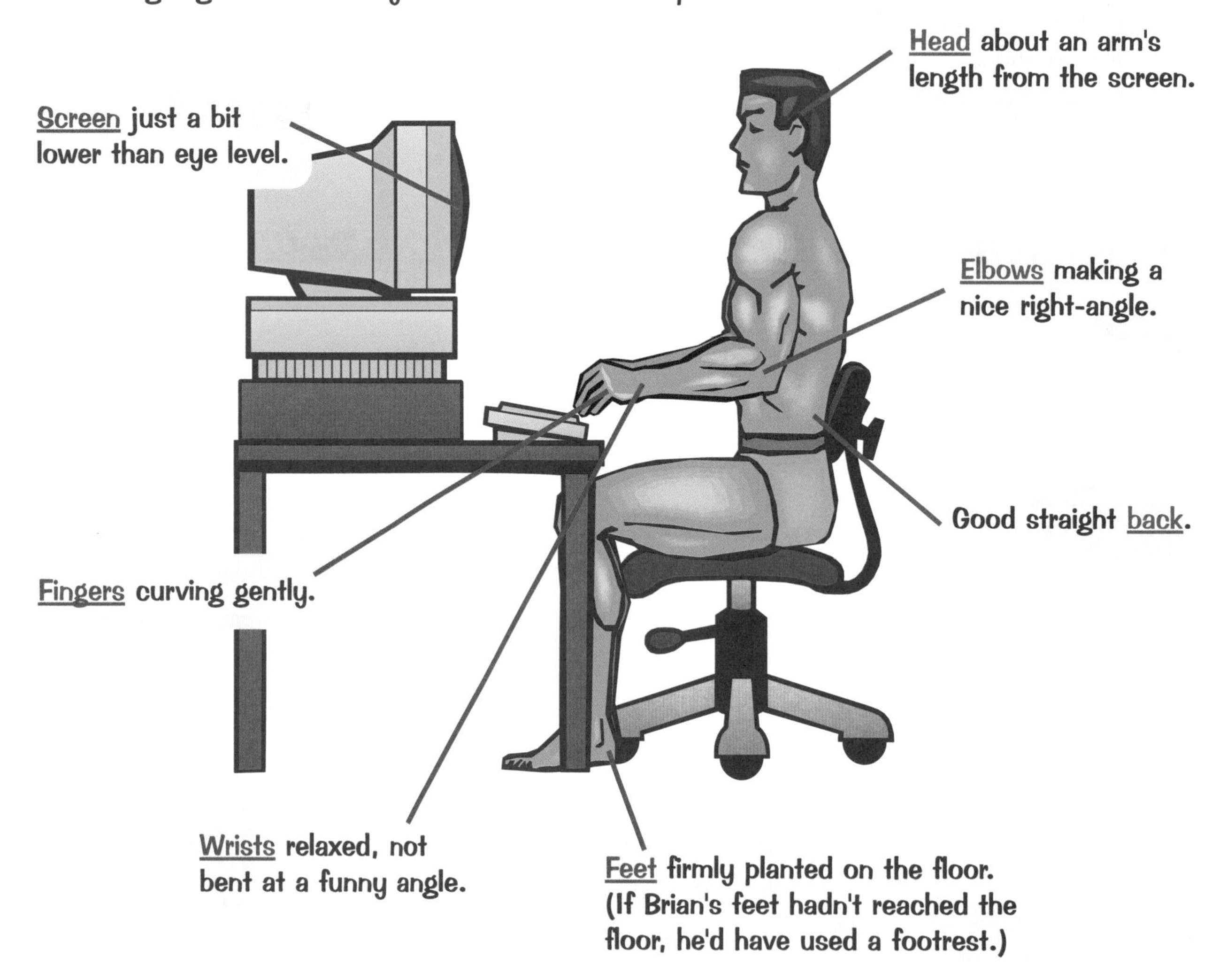

You might think all this advice is a bit silly, but there's good reason for it:

1) Using a computer for long periods of time can cause RSI (Repetitive Strain Injury) or WRULD (Work-Related Upper Limb Disorder). It's where you damage your nerves by making lots of small repetitive movements, and they really hurt.
2) You can also give yourself back and neck problems by sitting the wrong way for a long time.
3) These problems are hard to get rid of once you've got them, so the best advice is to try not to get them — and that means sitting properly.

Difficult stuff this — bum on chair, feet on floor...

Spending a long time sitting in an unhealthy position can hurt — simple as that.
So don't ignore this advice, or you might find computers a pain in more ways than one.

Computer Health and Safety

There are a few more things you should learn to make sure you're healthy and safe.

Set Up Your Workstation Properly

But what's a workstation?

Your workstation is your desk, and all the computer-related things on it that you might need when you're working, e.g. keyboard, mouse, printer, cup of tea.

To prevent RSI and nasty straining problems, you should set your workstation up so that you can sit properly and reach everything without having to stretch or strain:

1) The keyboard should be just below elbow-level, so that you can type without needing to bend your wrists back. It should also be kept flat (with its little legs folded up).
2) The mouse and keyboard should be within easy reach.
3) There should be plenty of room to move the mouse about freely — so no desk clutter.
4) The monitor should be between 18 and 24 inches away, and right in front of you, rather than at an angle. You should also make sure there's no glare on the screen from a window or light. Glare is really annoying and can strain your eyes.

Don't Work Too Hard

Another good tip for avoiding health problems is to take regular breaks. Don't keep slogging away non-stop at your keyboard — it'll only make you hurt.

Try to take a little break about every 20 minutes — make sure you have a stretch and walk about.

Brian won't get RSI.

And stretch, two, three, and type, two, three...

You're not likely to get computer-related problems if you only use a computer occasionally. So don't panic about RSI too much — this is just a warning so you know.

Turn your Computer On and Off

Before you go any further, you need to know how to turn your computer on and off.

All you have to do is Press Two Buttons

You usually have to turn on your computer and your monitor separately.

Turn on the computer.
When you push this switch, you'll hear lots of whirring noises as the computer gets going.

It takes a while for all the programs on your computer to load. You'll probably see a log-in screen (see page 11) when it's ready.

Turn on the monitor.
The button is usually just below the screen.

You need to 'Shut Down' your Computer Properly

'Shutting Down' lets the computer sort out its files before it switches off — like someone tidying their desk before leaving work.

Find the button on your screen that says 'Start' — this is the 'Start menu'.
Click on it with your left mouse button and then move the mouse until 'Shut down' is highlighted. Click again.

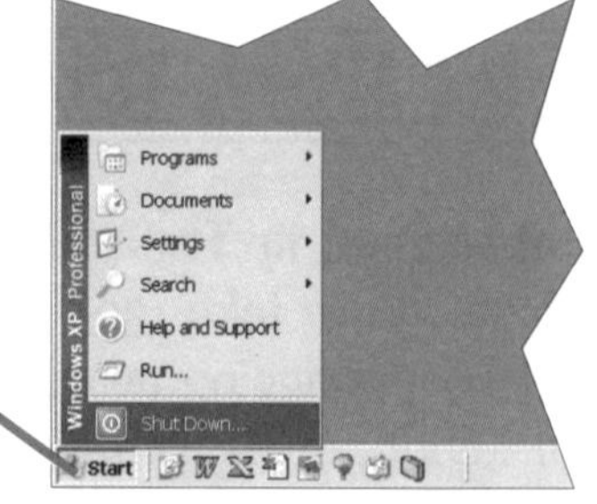

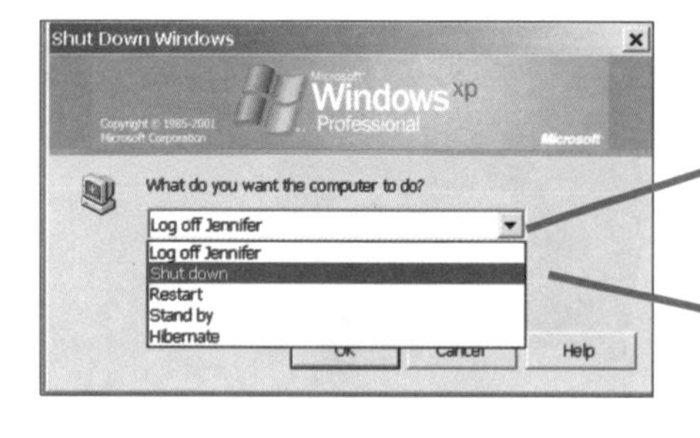

Click on this arrow.

3 You should see a box that looks a bit like this on your screen. Select 'Shut down' then click 'OK'.

The computer will go off by itself after a few seconds. Turn off the monitor by pressing the button on the front, just like you did to turn it on. Easy peasy.

Switching on and off is a nice easy start...

It might seem a bit of a waste of time, but it's worth turning your computer on and off just to make sure you know how to do it. It's as easy as turning on your TV.

How to Log On and Off

You might have to log on to your computer and log off when you've finished using it.
Why? How? — well read on...

Logging On tells the Computer Who You Are

Some computers are used by lots of people.
They need you to 'log on', so they can identify each user.
It also helps make things more secure.

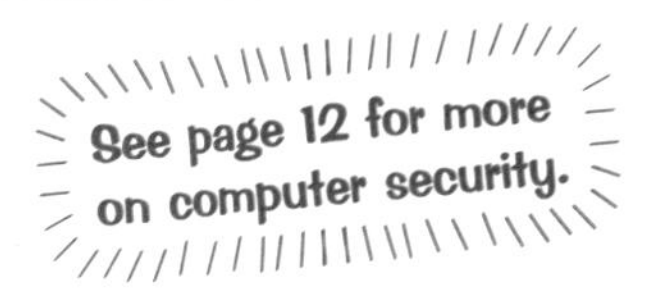

How you log on can vary a lot, so get your tutor to show you exactly how to do it on your college computers.
You may see something like this when you start using the computer:

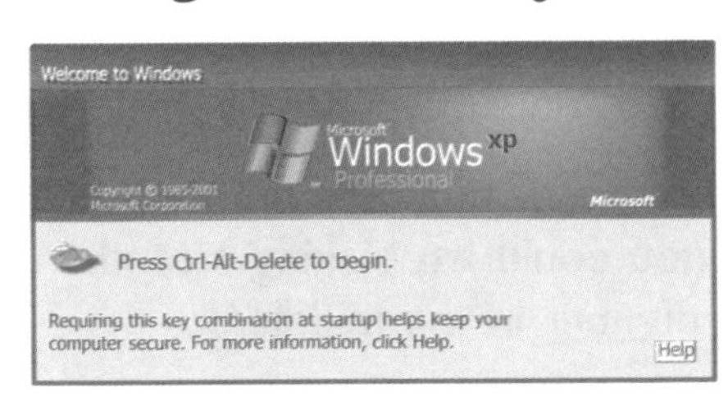

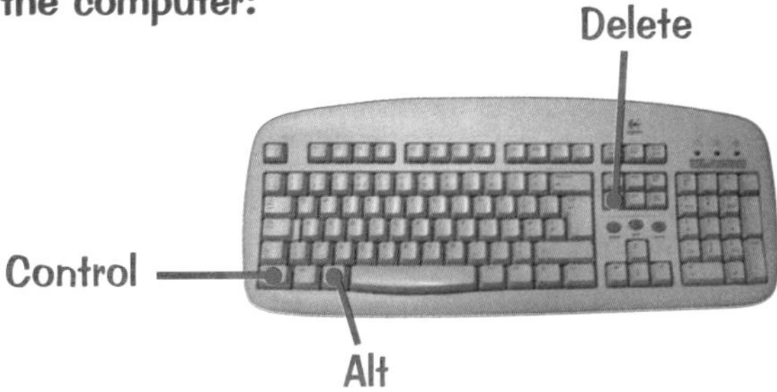

Hold down the 'Ctrl' key on your keyboard, and at the same time press the 'Alt' key and the 'Delete' key.
Keep them all pressed down at once, (use three fingers).

Click in the box where it says 'User name' and type your user name.

Click in the box where it says 'Password' and type your password.

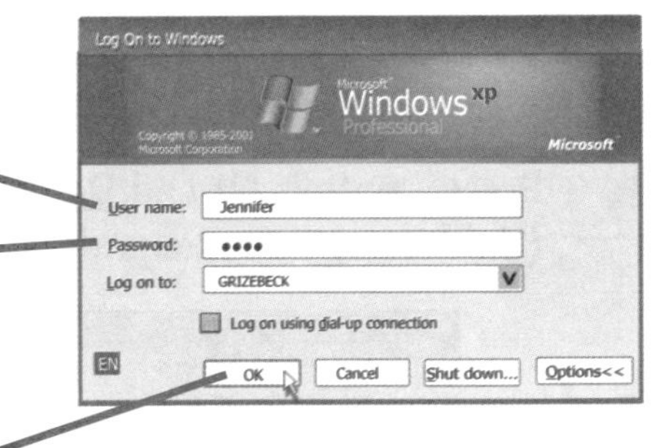

Ask your tutor to tell you your username and password

Then click on 'OK' with the mouse.
Now you're logged in and ready to work.

If you're unsure about entering text, see page 20.

Log Off or Shut Down when you've Finished

To log off, you go to the 'Start' menu as if you're going to Shut Down, (see page 10).
At stage 2, select 'log off' instead of 'shut down', then click 'OK'.

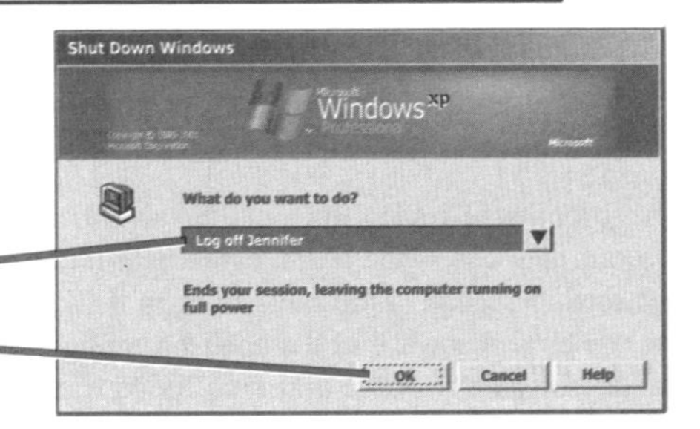

Don't forget your password...

Make sure you learn the logging-on procedure for your college computers.
The next page has more about passwords and why we bother to use them.
You'll learn how to change your password into something you're more likely to remember.

Passwords

So you know how to enter a password — but why bother having one? Ah, well, read on...

Passwords are Excellent for Security

Here's why passwords are so important:

> Passwords stop other people from getting on your computer and reading private things or messing about with your work.

Passwords are only good security if you choose them wisely. Here's how:

1) Don't have an obvious password that people can guess.
   This means avoiding your name, your pet's name, your favourite football team, etc.
2) The best password is a completely random mixture of numbers and letters, but this would be really hard to remember. Instead, you could try picking a random word from the dictionary, or having a word with a number in the middle.
3) Whatever password you choose, remember to change it quite often — at least once a month.

....and of course don't tell anyone your password...

Changing your Password is Easy

Seeing as it's a good idea to change your password regularly, you should probably learn how:

Press Control, Alt and Delete.
(Hold these three keys down at the same time.)

This process depends a lot on how your computer is set up, so if Control, Alt and Delete don't work, ask your tutor.

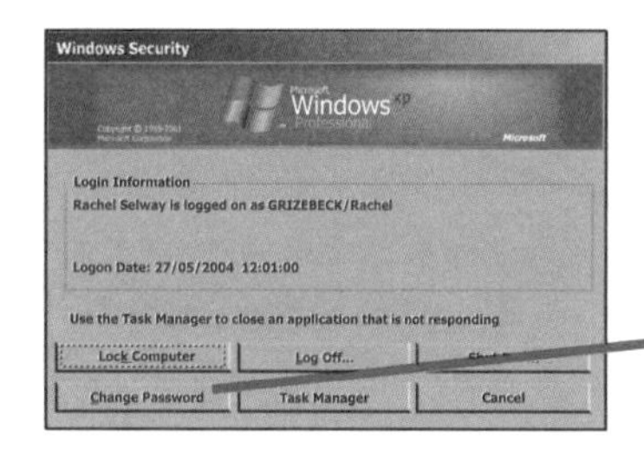

You'll get a little window like this. Click your mouse on the bit that says 'Change Password...'

You'll get another window. Click your mouse on the box next to 'Old Password'. Then type in your old password.

Click on the next box down, and type in your new password. Type in the new password again in the last box.

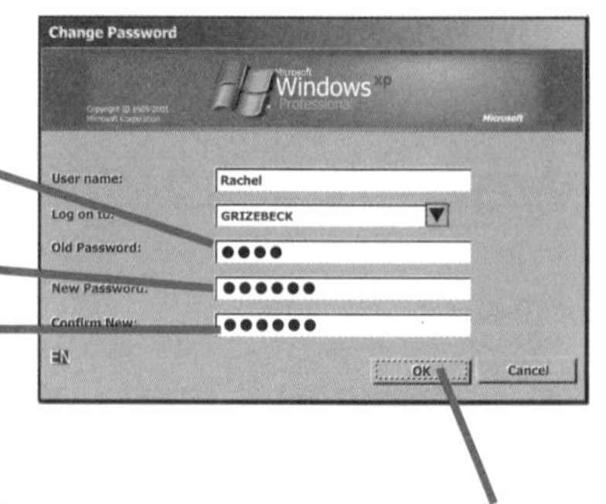

This process of typing your old password, then your new one twice is the same with most password changing. (You have to type it twice so the computer knows that it's spelt correctly — it wouldn't be able to tell if you only typed it once.)

Click your mouse on 'OK'. And it's all done.

'Password' is also not the best password...

When you type in your password, it'll appear as little circles. This is so that nobody can read it over your shoulder. Clever, eh? You've got to remember your password to get onto your computer but don't write it on a post-it note stuck to your monitor — that would just be silly.

Computer Security

The work on your computer won't be totally safe unless you take a few precautions...

There are a Few Ways You Might Lose Your Work...

1) If your computer breaks, you might lose all your work and the information stored on it.
2) Things like power cuts can cause problems too. If you work on something without saving it, and then the electricity goes off, you'll have lost it. Oops.

Trust no-one.

3) Some people invent viruses which travel from computer to computer, deleting files, or generally messing things about. These people invent viruses for a laugh. But it's not funny.
4) Small children enjoy playing with things they don't understand, dogs enjoy eating disks, guinea pigs enjoy chewing wires, tea enjoys getting spilt all over your keyboard.

...But Take Precautions and You'll be Fine

Don't be scared — it's easy not to lose your work if you follow some simple rules:

Have a password so that only you can use your computer (see the previous page).

When you're working, save, save and save again. Keep saving. Save every five minutes. Or more. You'll learn how to do this later in the book.

Keep extra copies of your work on a disk so that if you lose the copy on your computer, you'll have a spare. But keep your disks in a safe place too.

All computers should have some virus-finding software. This software won't let you open files if it thinks they're dodgy.

Just don't forget to save...

People worry that they can always lose work they do on computers, but a few simple precautions can save a world of frustration. The computer itself even helps you not to lose work. If you try to close without saving, it'll ask you if you're sure you don't want to save first.

Navigate the Operating System

The operating system is the program that organises all the other programs, so it's vital that you know how to use it.

Most Computers use Windows

There are all sorts of different operating systems, but most use things called windows. These are boxes on the screen that you can move around, resize or stack on top of one another. The most common operating system is called Microsoft Windows.

There's more about windows on page 15.

The Main Work Area is the Desktop

The desktop is what you see when you've switched on or logged on to your computer.

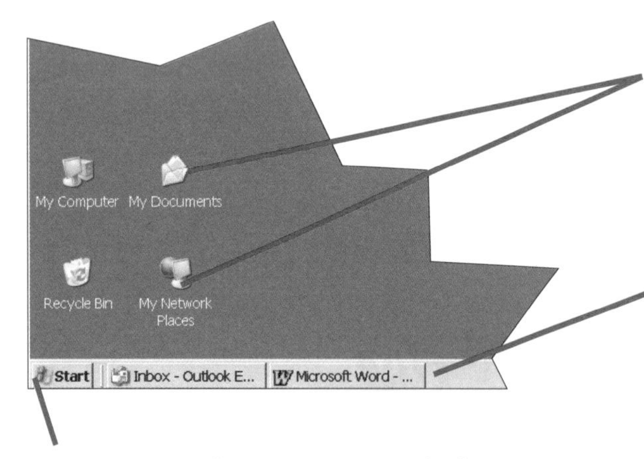

You've seen these icons before (little pictures which represent files or applications). You've also had a go at double-clicking them to open programs (see page 7 if you've forgotten).

This is the taskbar. It shows you which applications you have open at the moment. This computer has an email application, and a word-processing (writing) application open.

You've seen the 'Start menu' before. This is where you can shut down or log off, and also open most programs and documents.

There are Two very Important Icons on the Desktop

1) 'My Computer' lets you get at the parts of the computer where information is stored (the disk drives). This is where you can find things you've created and saved.

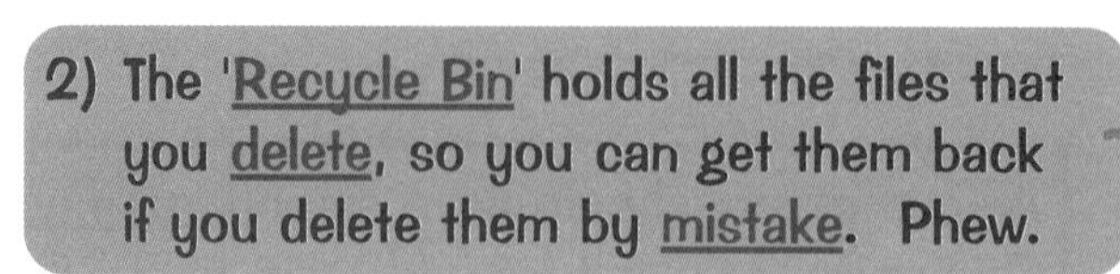

2) The 'Recycle Bin' holds all the files that you delete, so you can get them back if you delete them by mistake. Phew.

The desktop has most of the things you need...

You're going to see a lot of the desktop. It's like a base camp on a mountain expedition (without the tents and primitive toilets). You go there at the beginning and the end of your expedition, and use it to access more exciting places in between.

Navigate the Operating System

All Windows have Similar Features

Here's an example of a typical window. This is what you'd see if you opened Microsoft Word.

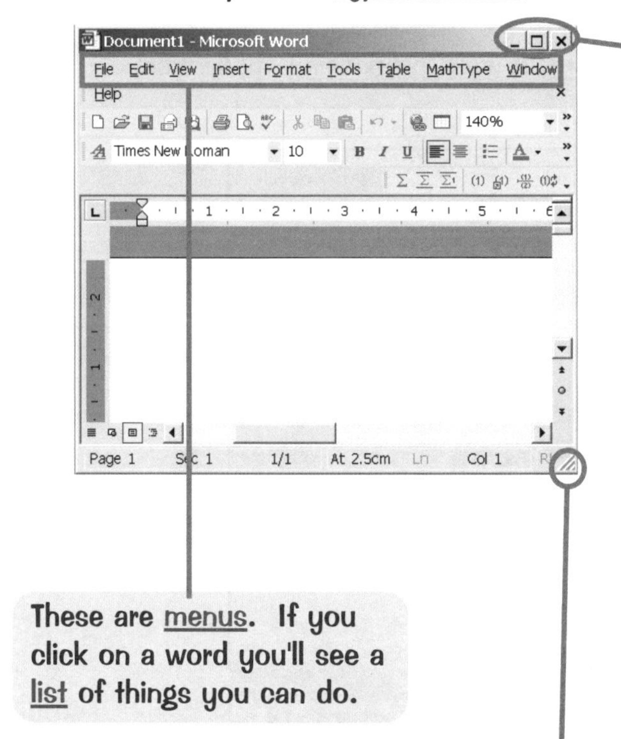

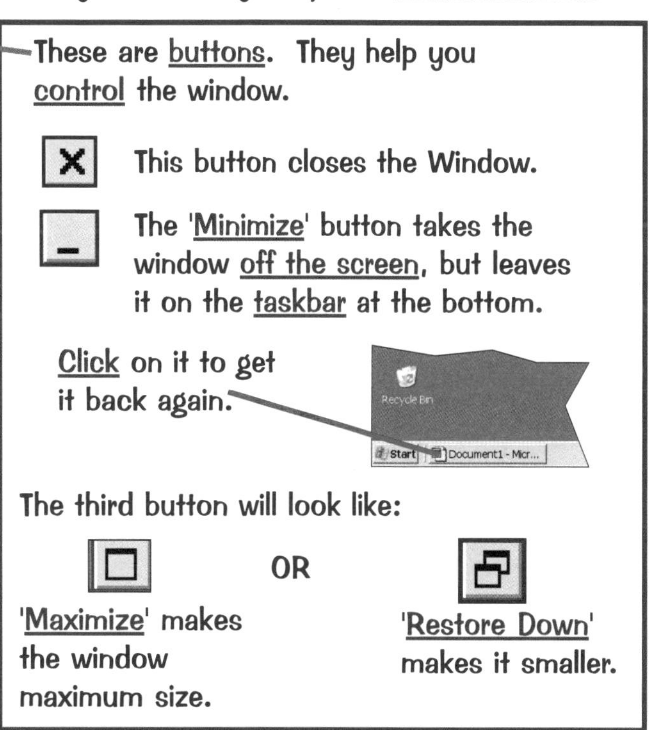

These are buttons. They help you control the window.

This button closes the Window.

The 'Minimize' button takes the window off the screen, but leaves it on the taskbar at the bottom.

Click on it to get it back again.

The third button will look like:

'Maximize' makes the window maximum size.

OR

'Restore Down' makes it smaller.

These are menus. If you click on a word you'll see a list of things you can do.

If you move the mouse over this corner the pointer will change into a two headed arrow. Click on the corner, hold the button down and move the mouse to 'resize' — make the window bigger or smaller. (You can't do this if it is maximised.)

You can Move Inside the Window

Sometimes the window doesn't show you all the information inside it, e.g. if you're looking at a letter with three pages, you'll only see part of the first page in the window.

You can move around it using the 'scroll bars' on the side and bottom of the window.

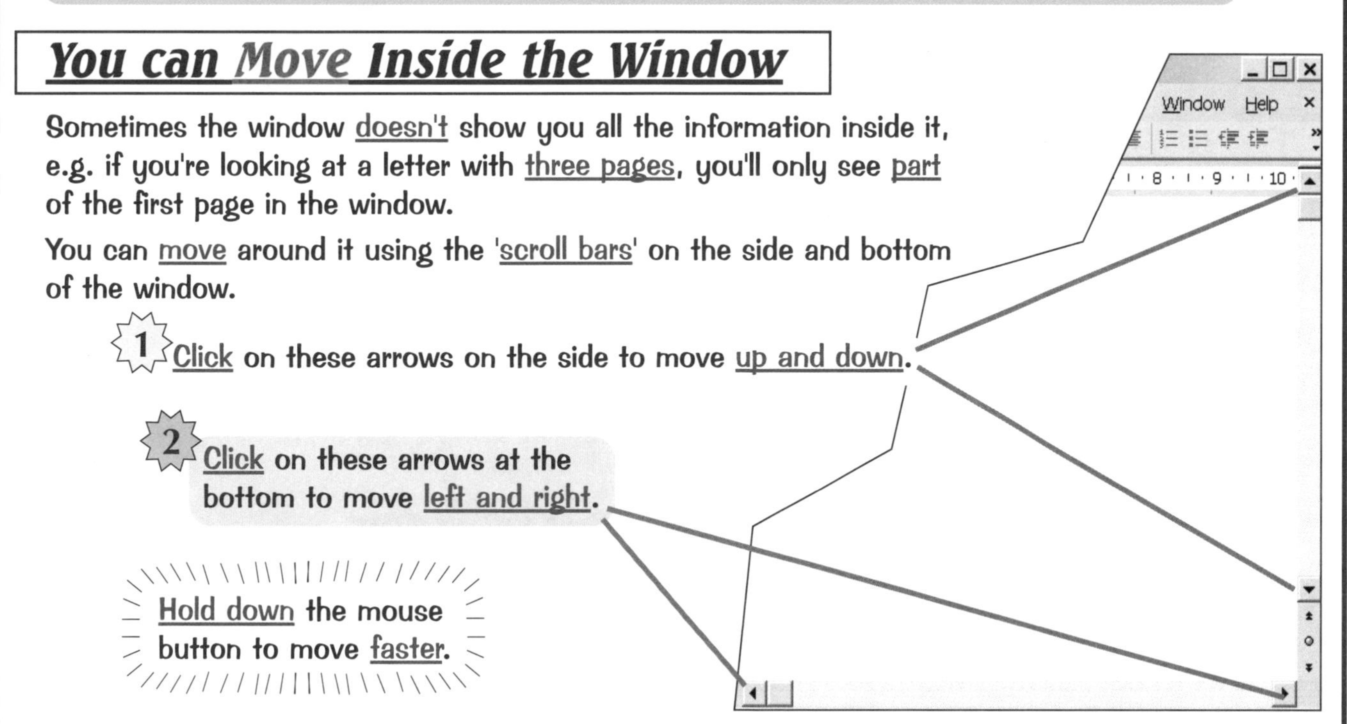

1. Click on these arrows on the side to move up and down.
2. Click on these arrows at the bottom to move left and right.

Hold down the mouse button to move faster.

You can make a window any size you want...

Try resizing and moving in a window until you're comfortable with the controls. It's really useful when you're using more than one program at a time.

Loading an Application

You're probably getting bored of the desktop by now, so it's time to start loading applications. (Don't forget — an application is just another word for a program.)

You can find Programs in the Start Menu

Imagine you want to write a letter using Microsoft Word, a word-processing application. Follow these steps to open the application.

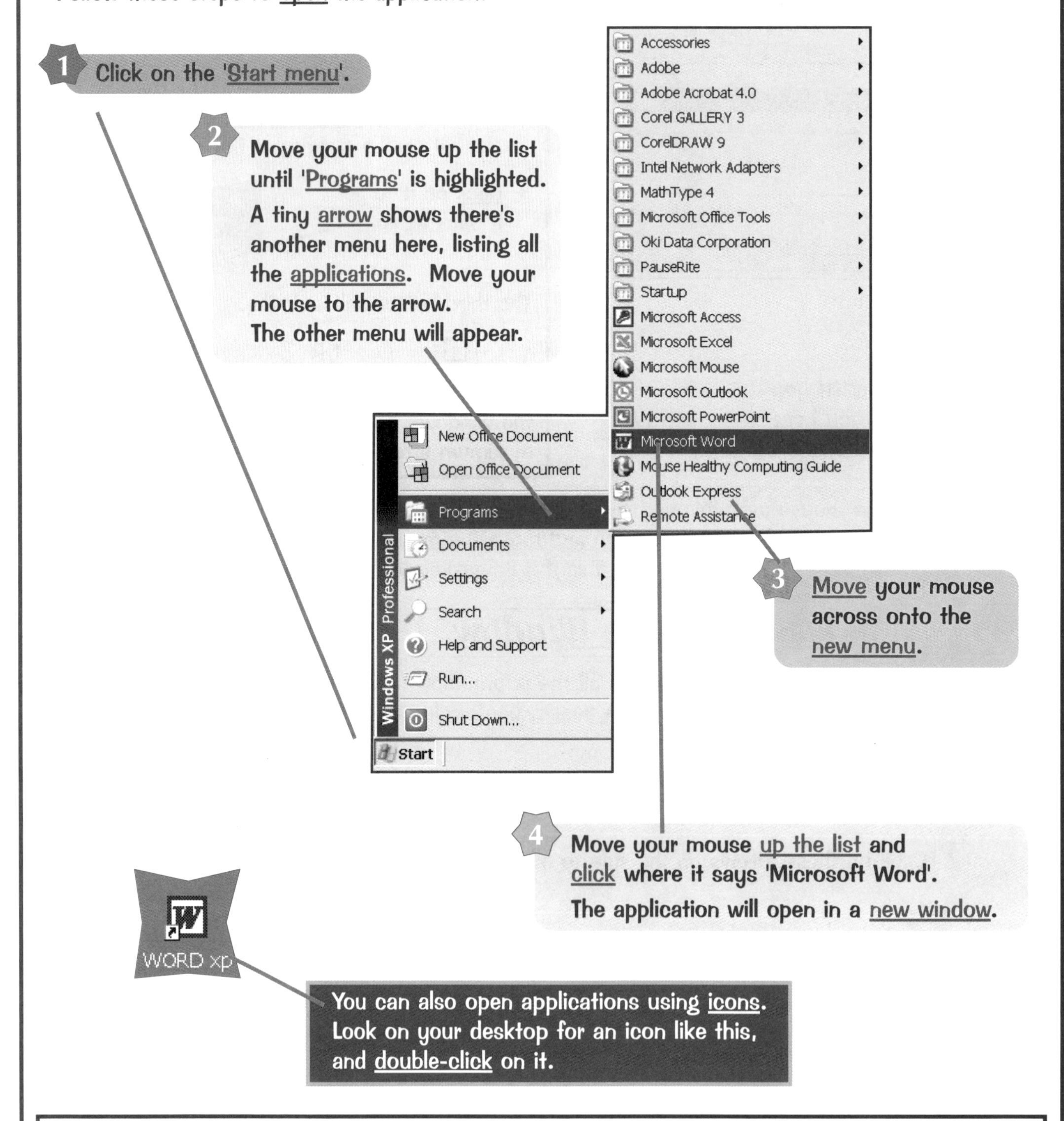

You can have lots of applications open at once...

One of the best things about Windows is that you can have lots of different applications open in lots of different windows. So you can check your email, write a letter, and play games all more or less at the same time.

Creating a New Document

Your Screen should Look Like This

You've opened a new window. Microsoft Word will have automatically created a new document (just like a paper document) and named it Document1.
You'll learn how to change document names later.

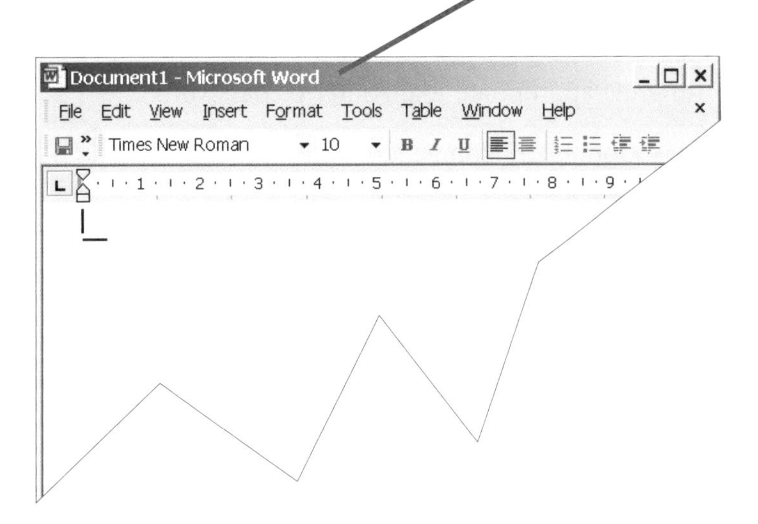

You can Open More than One Document at a Time

Try opening a second document.

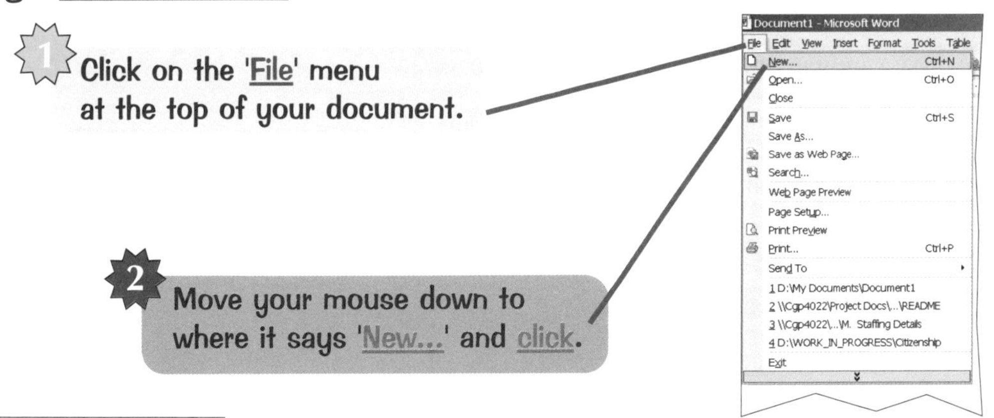

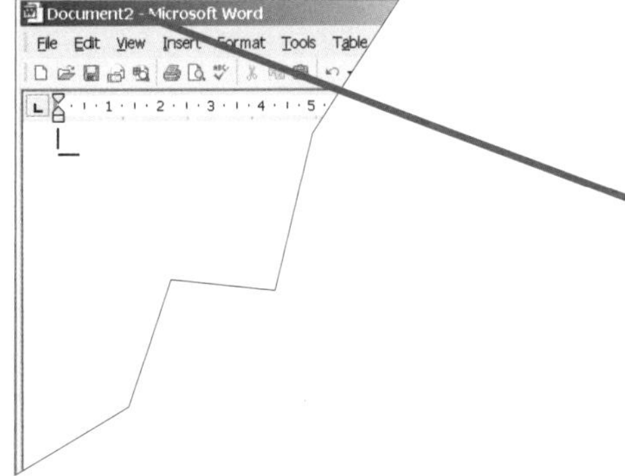

And there you have it. A new document.
It's called Document2 this time.
Don't worry — Document1 is still there as well, this new document has just been opened and put on top.

Now you're ready to write your life story...

You should be feeling a bit more familiar with windows now.
Don't be afraid to click on things to see what happens...

Section Two — Practice Exercises

The exercises on these two pages will give you good practice of everything you've learnt so far.

Exercise 1

1. Switch on the computer and monitor correctly and safely.
   Wait for the operating system software to load fully.
2. Access the system using the appropriate login and / or password.
3. Double-click on the 'My Computer' icon.
4. Double-click on 'Local Disk (C:)', to view the contents of the hard disk.
5. Click on the 'Maximize' button so that the 'Local Disk (C:)' window fills the entire screen (unless your window is already maximised).
6. Click the 'Minimize' button to take the window off the screen.
7. Click the 'Local Disk (C:)' button on the taskbar to reopen the window.
8. Close the window.

Exercise 2

1. Click on the 'Start' button.
2. Move your mouse onto the 'Programs' menu.
3. Move your mouse onto the 'Accessories' menu.
4. Click on the 'Calculator' application to open it.
5. Try out the following calculation 565 – 476 = ?
6. Minimize the calculator application.
7. Click on the 'Start' button.
8. Move your mouse onto the 'Programs' menu.
9. Click on the 'Microsoft Word' application to open it.
10. Click on the 'Minimize' button of Microsoft Word.
11. Click the 'Calculator' button on the taskbar to reopen the calculator application.
12. Click on the 'Microsoft Word' button on the taskbar to return to Word.
13. Close Microsoft Word.
14. Close the calculator application.
15. Click on the 'Start' button.
16. Select 'Shut Down...' from the options box, then 'OK' to shut down the computer.

Section Two — Practice Exercises

Another two to go... Remember — doing lots of practice like this is the best way to learn.

Exercise 3

1. Switch on the computer and monitor correctly and safely.
   Wait for the operating system software to load fully.
2. Gain access to your system using the appropriate login and / or password.
3. Double-click on the 'My Computer' icon.
4. Double-click on the 'Local Disk (C:)', to view the contents of the hard disk.
5. Click on the 'Maximize' button so that the 'Local Disk (C:)' window fills the entire screen (unless your window is already maximised).
6. Click on the 'File' menu.
7. Move your mouse onto the 'New' menu, then click on 'Folder' to create a new folder.
8. Type in your name as the new folder's name, then press 'Enter' on the keyboard.
9. Click the 'Restore' button to return the window to its previous size.
10. Close the window.

Exercise 4

1. Click on the 'Start' button.
2. Move your mouse onto the 'Programs' menu.
3. Click on the 'Microsoft Word' application.
4. Click on the 'Minimize' button of Microsoft Word.
5. Click on the 'Start' button, move onto the 'Programs' menu, then onto the 'Accessories' menu, then click on the 'Paint' application.
6. Have a play, using some of the tools on the left hand side to draw a picture.
   This will get you used to using the mouse.
7. Click on the 'Microsoft Word' button on the taskbar to return to Word.
8. Close Microsoft Word (if you are asked "Do you want to save the changes made to Document1?" click on the 'No' button).
9. Close the 'Paint' application (if you are asked "Do you want to save the changes made to untitled?" click on the 'No' button).
10. Click on the 'Start' button.
11. Click on 'Shut Down...', then 'OK' to shut down the computer.

Entering Text, Numbers and Symbols

Whether you're writing a letter or searching the Internet for holiday deals, you'll need to be able to enter text, numbers and symbols.

To Enter a letter, you just press a Key

1 Open up your word processing application — it's probably Microsoft Word. (You need to use the Start menu — see pages 16 and 17 if you've forgotten how.)

2 Press A ... you've entered the letter a

3 Press M ... you've entered the letter m

you get the idea... pretty simple so far.

The Enter Key takes you onto a New Line

4 Now press the Enter key.
It might say Enter on it or it might look like this:

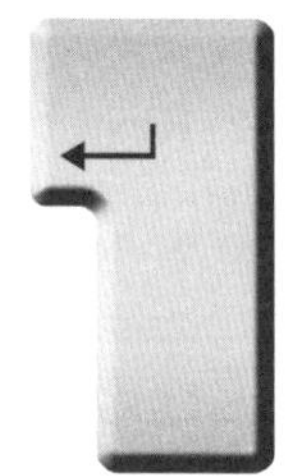

... this will end the line you are typing and take you onto a new line.

5 Type the word guinea

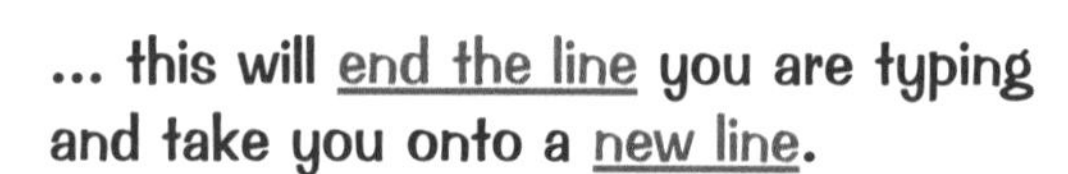

The Space Bar... well ... makes a Space

6 Press the space bar. It's the long thin one at the bottom of the keyboard. You use it to get the spaces between words.

7 Now type the word pig

If everything has gone according to plan your screen should look something like this:

Watch out — new versions of Word try to help you out by predicting when you need capital letters, so it might have made the letters 'a' and 'g' into capitals. Your tutor can turn 'AutoCorrect' off to solve this problem.

Fear not — it's really just like a typewriter...

Computer geeks love to give things fancy names like "inputting data". It might sound high-tech but it just means pressing keys. Don't be put off — have a go.

Entering Text, Numbers and Symbols

There are loads of other symbols you can get from the keyboard.
You need to know: = - / # . , : @ ? ! £ & % + * — good eh.

Shift has Two really important uses...

For the exercises on this page open a word processing document to practise in (see p 16 and 17).

1 — Shift can make Capital Letters

1. Press the Shift key and keep it held down. It looks like this: 

2. At the same time press  . You'll get A instead of a.

2 — Shift can make Punctuation marks and Special Symbols

You'll see that the number keys also have symbols on them...

To make the symbol hold down Shift and press the number.

1. Hold down SHIFT and press 1 — you'll get !. Clever.

Some other keys also have symbols floating at the top of them.
Shift can get these too.

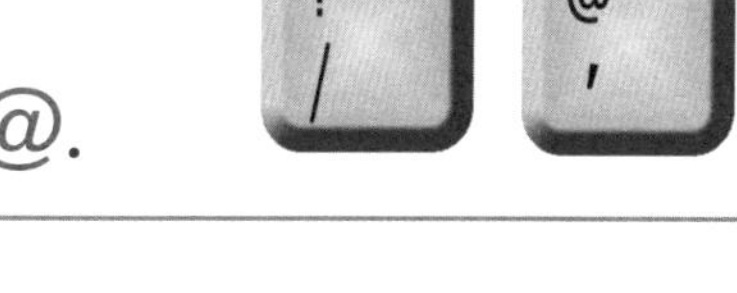

 2. Hold down SHIFT and press / — you'll get ?.

 3. Hold down SHIFT and press ' — you'll get @.

Caps Lock makes all the letters you type into Capitals

1. Press the Caps Lock key (on the left hand side of the keyboard).
There's normally a little light on the keyboard to show you the lock is on.

2. Type the word apple. Instead of apple it will come out as APPLE.
So if you want all the letters to be capitals, just put the Caps Lock on.
To turn it off again, you just press Caps Lock again.

The Control key is for things called Shortcuts

1) The Control key (Ctrl) has special functions.
2) For example in most programs if you hold down Ctrl and press S, the program will automatically save the document you are working on.
3) You don't need to worry about Ctrl — as long as you know what it does.

I'm afraid you've got to learn these b*#@*y symbols...

It sounds silly but it can take a bit of time to get used to using Shift. Remember to keep it held down whilst you press the other keys. But with a little practice you'll soon get the hang of it.

How to Change Text in a Document

If you write a letter on the computer, the beauty is that you can go back to the letter and make changes like adding in words, correcting mistakes etc...

You Can Select a point in the text with the Mouse

With the mouse you can click in the text where you want to edit.

As an example, get your tutor to open the document called "examplewords".

1. Move the mouse until the pointer is just before the word "writing".

2. Then click the left mouse button. The cursor will appear where you clicked.

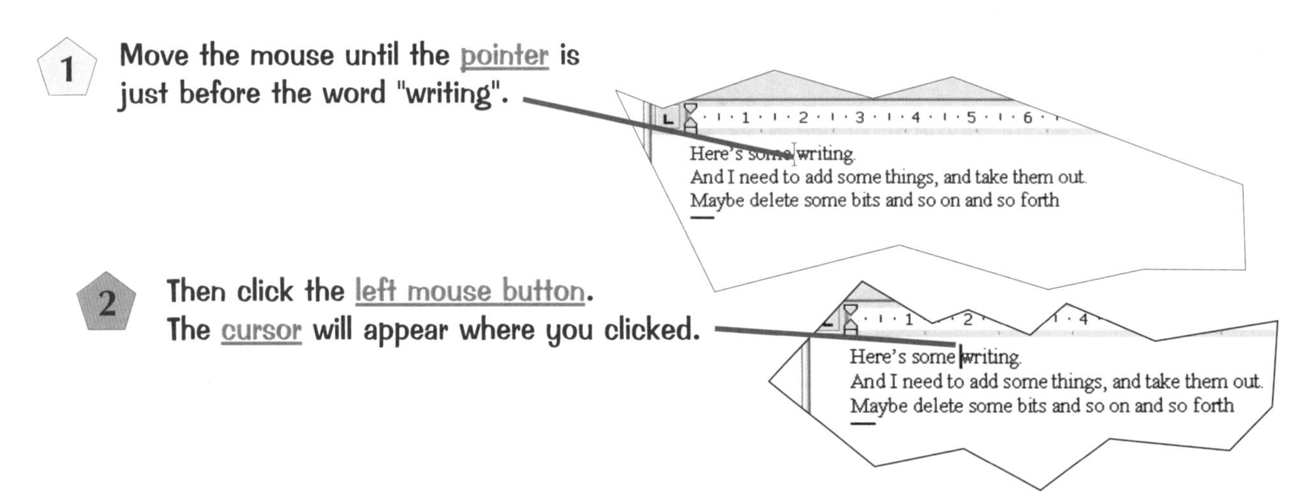

3. Now you can edit the text. Try adding the word 'boring' by just typing it in (don't forget the space).

You can Move through the text with the Cursor Keys

Remember the cursor keys (see page 4)...

...you can use them to move around the text until you get to the bit that you want to edit.

Have a go...

1. Use the mouse to click just before the word "Here's".
2. Use the cursor keys to move around the text until the cursor is after the comma in the second line.
3. Type the words "change some things". That's it — you've edited text.
4. Show your tutor and get them to close the file for you without saving.

I already did a swearing joke on the last page...

This editing malarky is a piece of cake. Click the mouse where you want to edit, move around with the cursor keys, type the odd word — what could be simpler.

How to Change Text in a Document

If you make a mistake you need to be able to go back and delete things...

The Backspace Key deletes Things

If you are typing and you realise that you have made a mistake,
the easiest way to fix it is often to use the Backspace key.
It might say Backspace on it or it might just look like this:

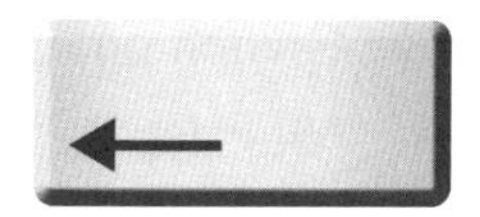

The Backspace key deletes the character BEHIND the cursor

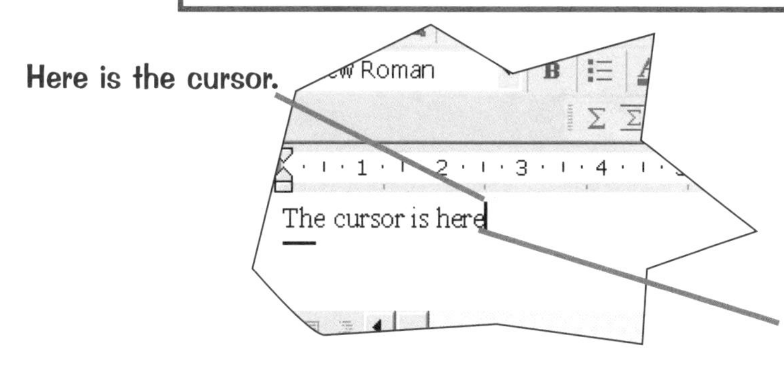

The Delete Key also deletes Stuff *(no surprise there...)*

Delete

The Delete key is similar. It normally says delete on it (sometimes just Del). It's over on the right-hand-side of the keyboard.

The Delete key deletes the character IN FRONT of the cursor

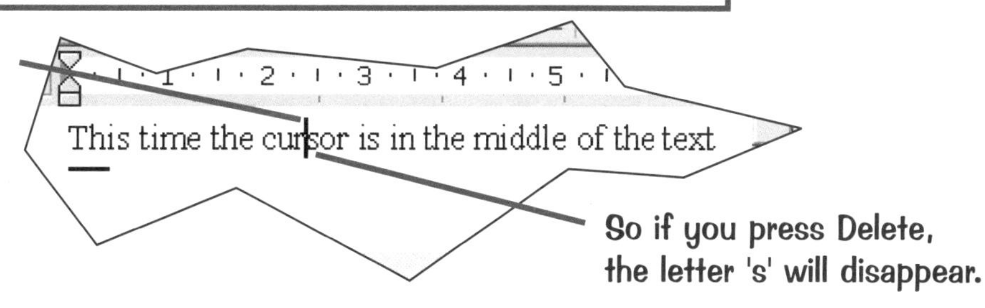

You Use All these Keys Together to Edit things

Have a quick go at this exercise to see if you've got the hang of it:

1 Get your tutor to open the document called "examplewords" again.

2 Use the mouse to put the cursor at the beginning of the first line. (Some programs might put it there automatically.)

3 Use the cursor keys and Backspace key to delete the words "and so forth".

4 Use the cursor keys and Delete key to delete the words "and take them out".

...or I'd make a joke about cursing keys...

Well that's that, entering text. To be honest it's all pretty easy, the main thing is just to get stuck in and have a go — you may be noticing it's a common theme.

Section Three — Practice Exercises

You should now be a whizz at entering data — let's see...

Exercise 1

1. Switch on the computer and monitor correctly and safely.
   Wait for the operating system software to load fully.
2. Create a new text document using a word processing application.
3. Enter the following data as shown, leaving a blank line between each line of text.

   results: 90.2% say "yes" / 9.8% say "no".

   Interest rates now @ 7.9% per year

   "Why am I doing this?" asked the student.

4. Leave another blank line then enter your name, centre number and today's date.
5. Close the application. Click on "no" when it asks you if you want to save.

The files used in these exercises have been included on a CD. If you are studying in a centre you'll need to ask your tutor where to get the files from. We haven't covered opening files yet so get your tutor to open it for you.

Exercise 2

1. Using an application that will allow you to read text files, open the file **memo1**.
2. Using the mouse and keyboard (or alternatives if available)
   add the following at the end of the text.

   Thank you for your co-operation.

3. Add your name, your centre number and today's date below the end of the text.
4. Close the application. Click on "no" when it asks you if you want to save.
5. Shut down your operating system correctly and safely.

Section Three — Practice Exercises

Don't worry if you struggled a bit with some of the last exercises.
Practice makes perfect and there's a whole load more practice to do here...

Exercise 3

1. Switch on the computer and monitor correctly and safely.
   Wait for the operating system software to load fully.
2. Create a new text document using a word processing application.
3. Enter the following data as shown, leaving space between each line.

   Eg. info know-how(2)

   Item Price (ID234#) @ £3.99

4. Leave another blank line then enter your name, centre number and today's date.
5. Close the application. Click on "no" when it asks you if you want to save.

Exercise 4

How to do this is covered later in the book. For now your tutor can help you open the file.

1. Using an application that will allow you to read text files, open the file **printers**.
2. Using the mouse and keyboard, add a blank line after the last line of text and then enter the following.

   There are only two printer types available now:

   Ink Jet
   Laser (Black & White or Colour)

3. Add your name, your centre number and today's date a few lines below the end of the text.
4. Close the application. Click on "no" when it asks you if you want to save.

Opening an Existing Document

You'll often want to open a document that already exists on your computer. Like if you've started writing a letter and you want to finish it.

You can Open a Document using the Application

To see how to open documents we are going to open a memo called 'July':

1. Open 'Microsoft Word' (see page 16).

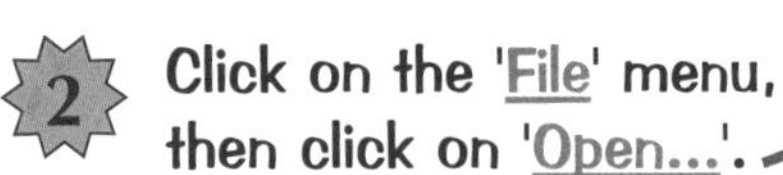

2. Click on the 'File' menu, then click on 'Open...'.

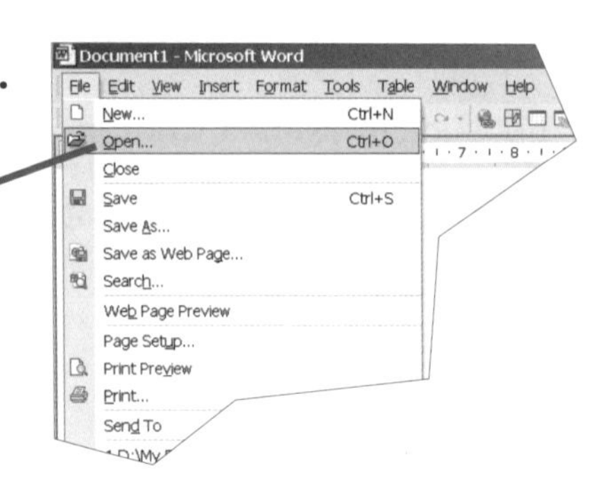

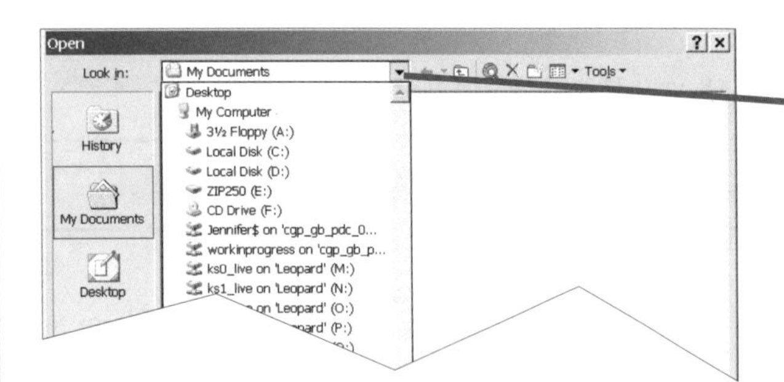

3. Click on this arrow and you'll get a list of all the places your files might be stored.

4. Move down and click on the place where the file has been stored.

We've included the files and folders you need on the CD. Ask your tutor where to find them on your computer.

5. You'll see a list of the files and folders in that part of the computer. Look for a folder called 'Reindeer Records' and double-click on it to open it.

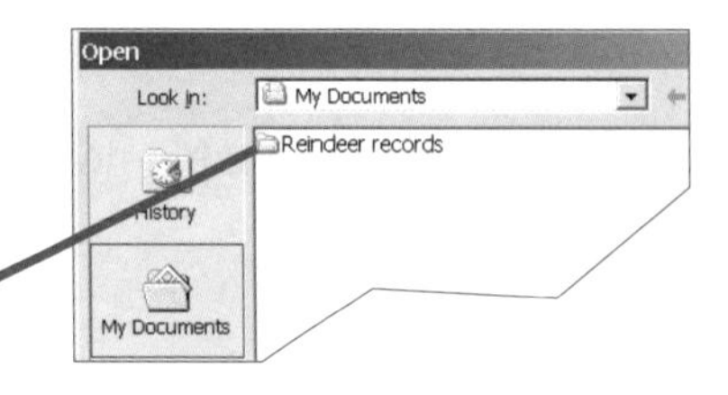

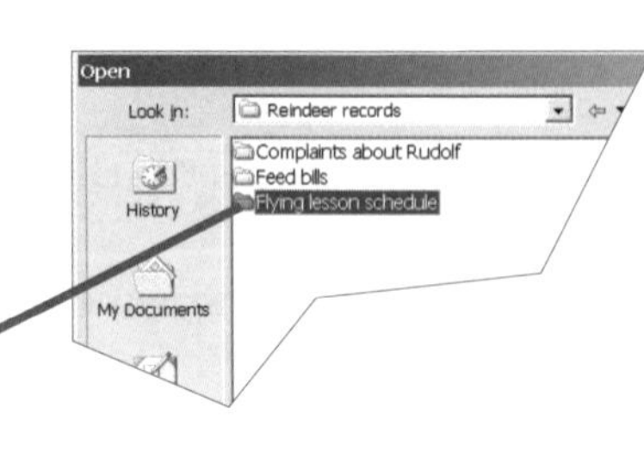

6. Now you can see the folders contained in 'Reindeer Records' Double-click on the 'Flying Lesson Schedule' folder.

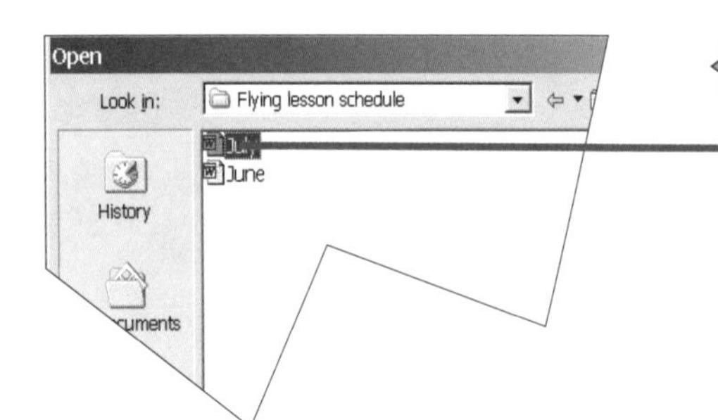

7. In there you'll find a file named 'July', double-click to open it.

It's a lot like an old-fashioned filing cabinet...

Files are stored in folders, and those folders are inside other folders, just like in a paper filing system. Each time you double-click on a folder it shows you what's in it.

Closing Documents

You've learnt how to open files, so here's a couple of ways to close them.

You can Close Files without Closing the Application

1 Click on this button to close the file without closing the whole application.

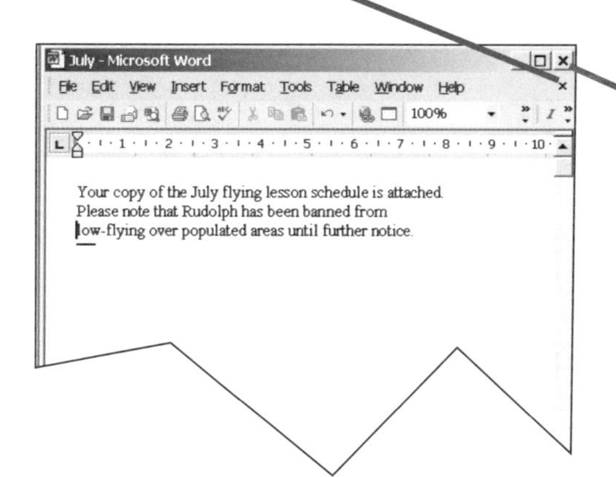

You've already learnt how to close the whole window using this button (see page 15).

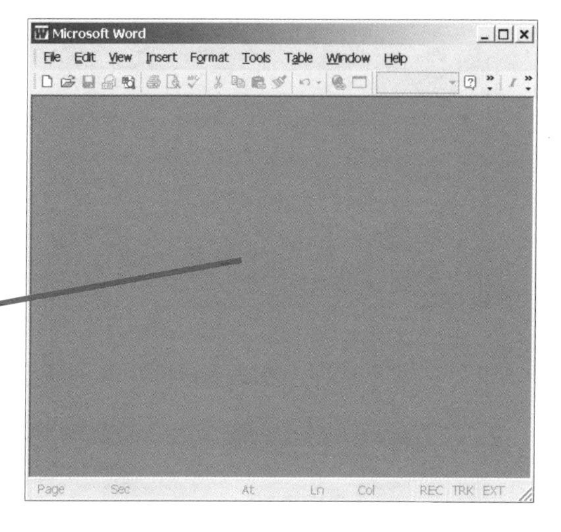

Now the window should look like this — you've got the application open, but no documents.

There's Another Way to Close Files

1 Open a file again (repeat what you did on page 26).

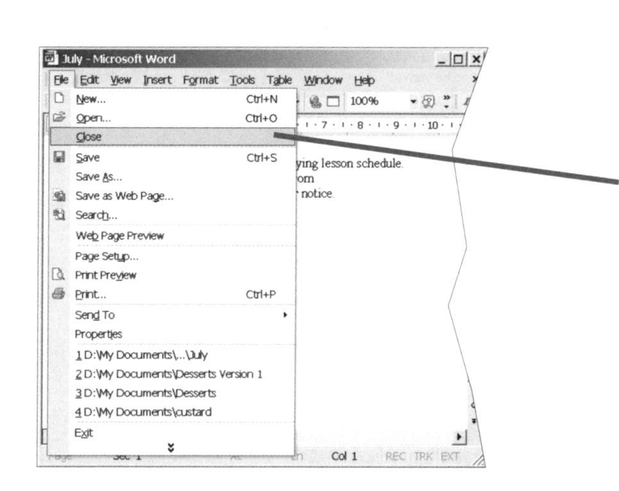

2 Click on the 'File' menu, move your mouse down and click on 'Close'.

Open and close a few things for practice...

There's often more than one way to do things on computers.
It might seem a bit confusing, but the nice thing is you can just learn the way you find easiest.

Saving a Document

Saving is a way of storing the document you are working on.
Once it is saved you can open and use it again whenever you want.

Here's How to Save your File

Create a new Microsoft Word document.
(see page 17 if you've forgotten). Type 'custard' in it.

Click on the 'File' menu, move down the menu and click on 'Save'.

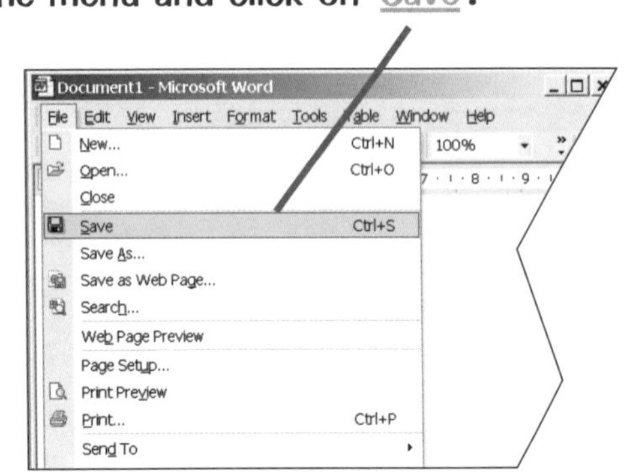

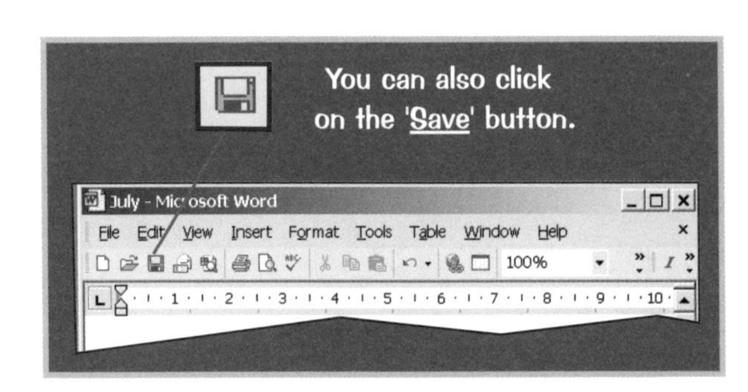

This screen lets you name your file, and choose where to save it.

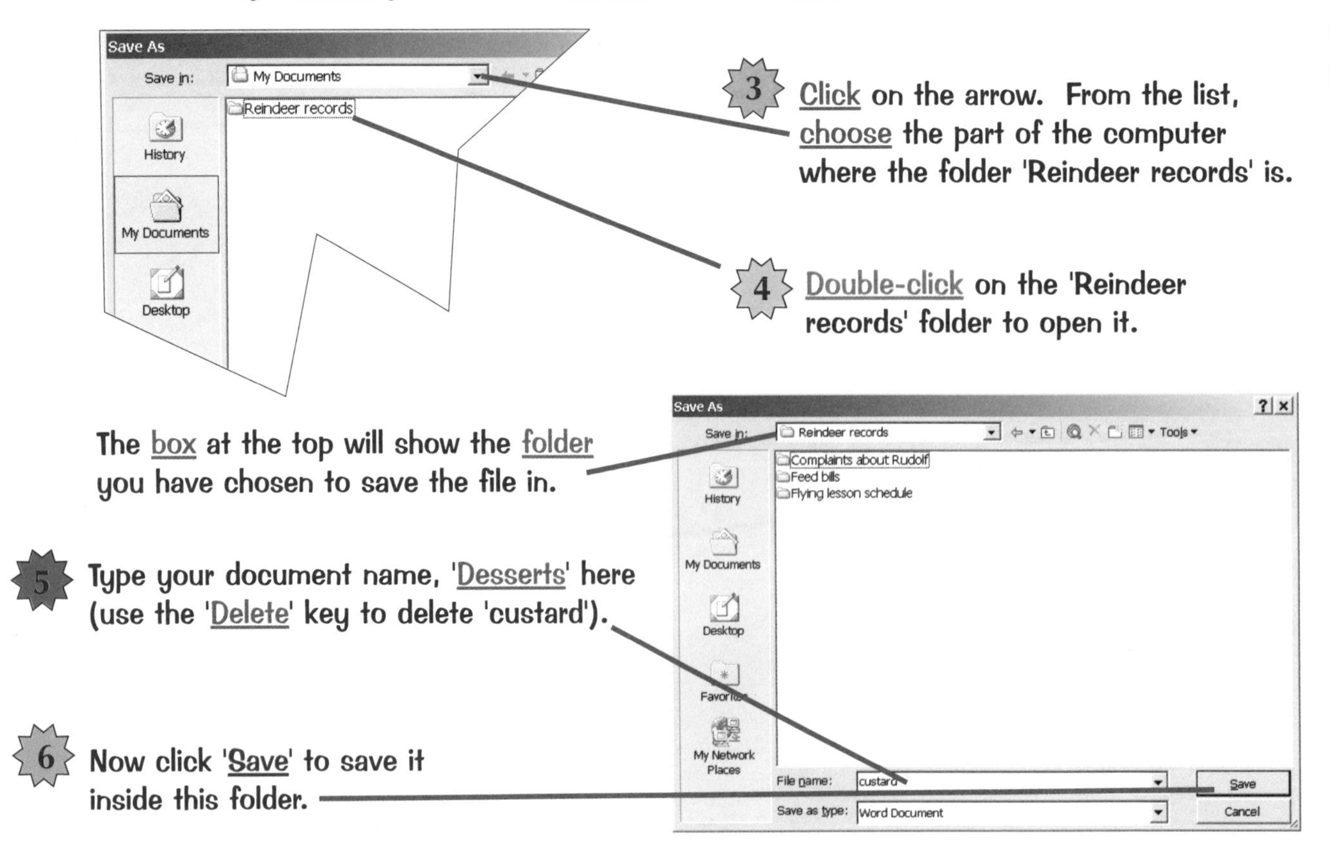

3 Click on the arrow. From the list, choose the part of the computer where the folder 'Reindeer records' is.

4 Double-click on the 'Reindeer records' folder to open it.

The box at the top will show the folder you have chosen to save the file in.

5 Type your document name, 'Desserts' here (use the 'Delete' key to delete 'custard').

6 Now click 'Save' to save it inside this folder.

Don't forget to save your files...

Get into the habit of saving the document you're working on every few minutes.
Otherwise if the computer 'crashes' you might lose your work.

Saving a Document

When you make changes to an existing document, you can choose whether to replace (overwrite) the old document when you save it.

'Save' Overwrites the Existing Document

Look at your document 'Desserts' from page 28. Type the word 'Jelly' on it.

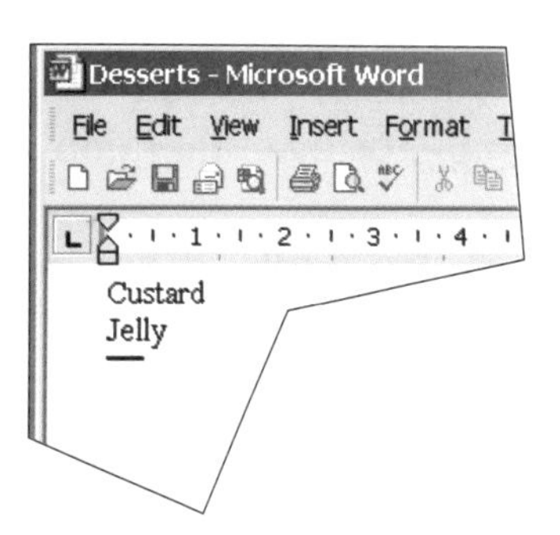

Save the document (see page 28).

The computer has saved your changes to the file. The original document (just saying 'Custard') no longer exists — it has been replaced by the new version.

'Save as' saves a New Version of an Existing Document

If you don't want to lose the original version of your document, you need to save the new version under a new name using the 'Save As...' button.

Add the words 'Ice-cream' to your document 'Desserts'.

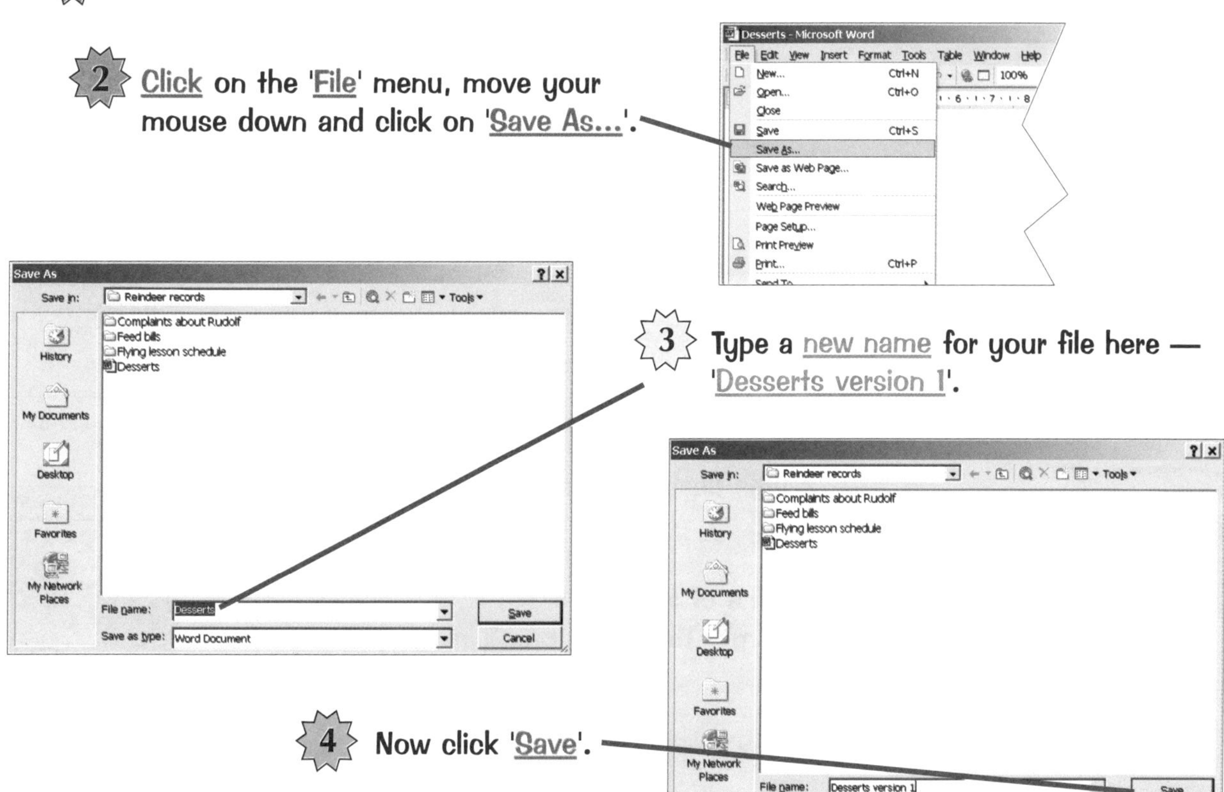

2. Click on the 'File' menu, move your mouse down and click on 'Save As...'.

3. Type a new name for your file here — 'Desserts version 1'.

4. Now click 'Save'.

You can save as many versions as you want...

It can be a good idea to save several versions of something if you're making changes to it. Then if you mess things up, you'll always have an older version to go back to.

Searching for Files

What happens if you can't remember where you stored a file? Panic? Nope — use 'Search'.

Finding Lost Files is Easy Using 'Search'

'Search' is a really useful tool for finding things on your computer. You can look for files, folders or applications with a certain name, of a certain type, or even that you saved on a certain day. Wow.

Search is called 'Find File' on some systems.

You can search for anything, but let's imagine you want to look for a Word file you remember is called 'letter to mum'. Here's how:

1. Click your left mouse button on 'Start' in the bottom left-hand corner of your screen.

2. A menu will appear. Move your mouse until the pointer rests on 'Search', which will be highlighted.

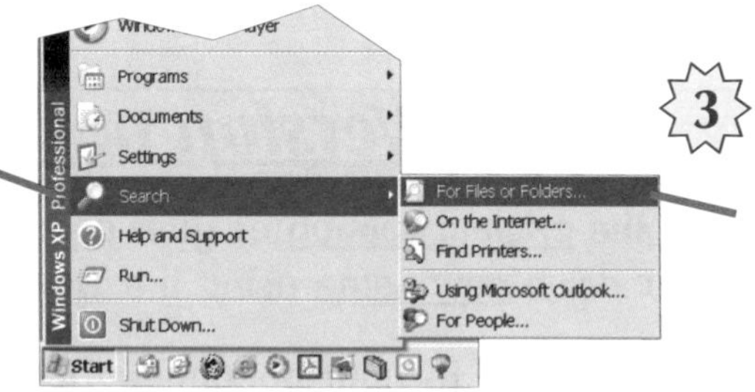

3. Move across to 'For Files or Folders...', then click your mouse again.

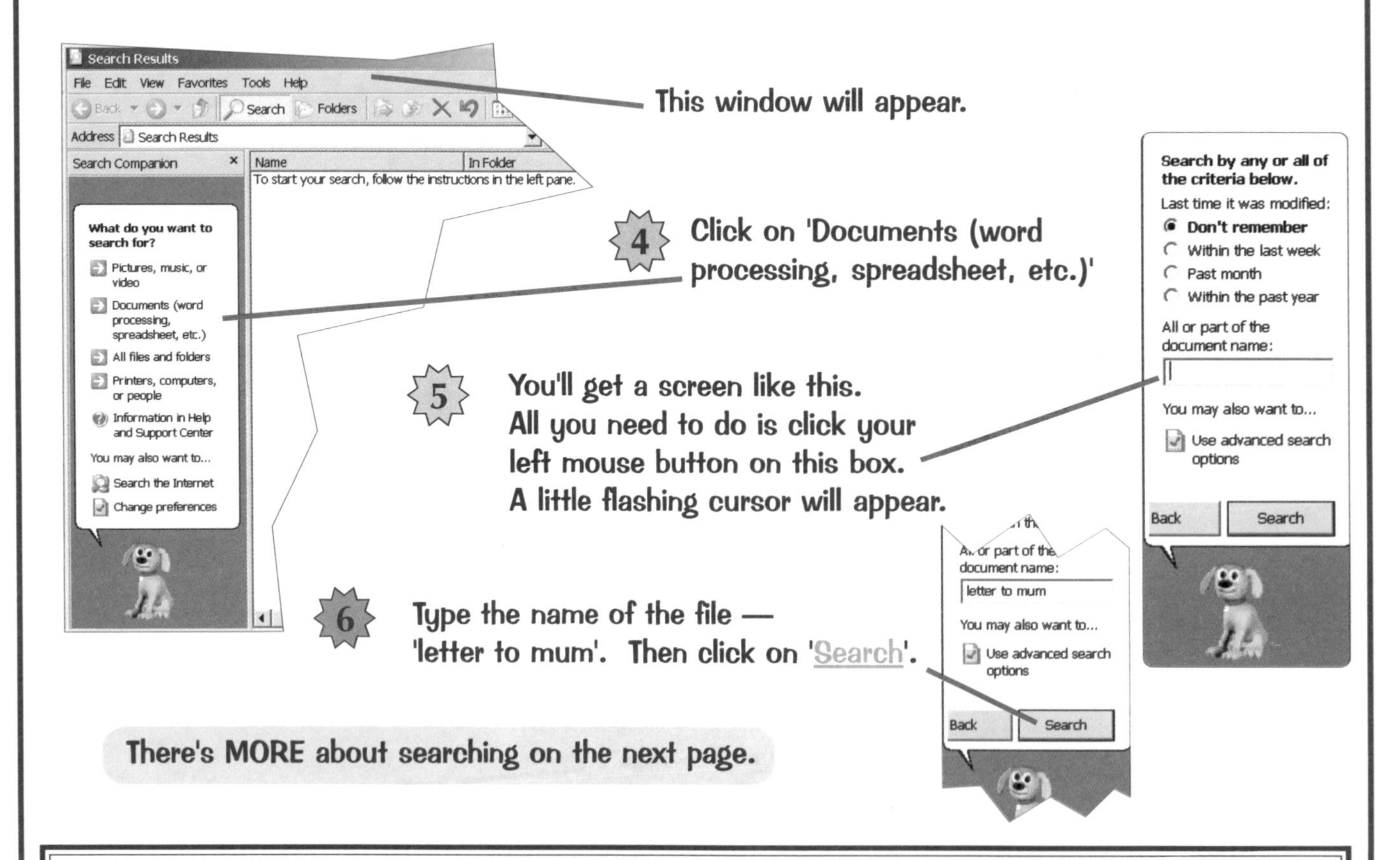

This window will appear.

4. Click on 'Documents (word processing, spreadsheet, etc.)'

5. You'll get a screen like this. All you need to do is click your left mouse button on this box. A little flashing cursor will appear.

6. Type the name of the file — 'letter to mum'. Then click on 'Search'.

There's MORE about searching on the next page.

Look at the next page for more on searching...

Here's a quick tip for searching — don't panic if you can't remember the name of the file you want. Search will find things even if you give it just part of the filename. So typing in 'letter', or 'mum', would be enough for it to find 'letter to mum'. Clever.

Searching for Files

And here's some more on how to search...

Your Computer will Keep Searching for Ages

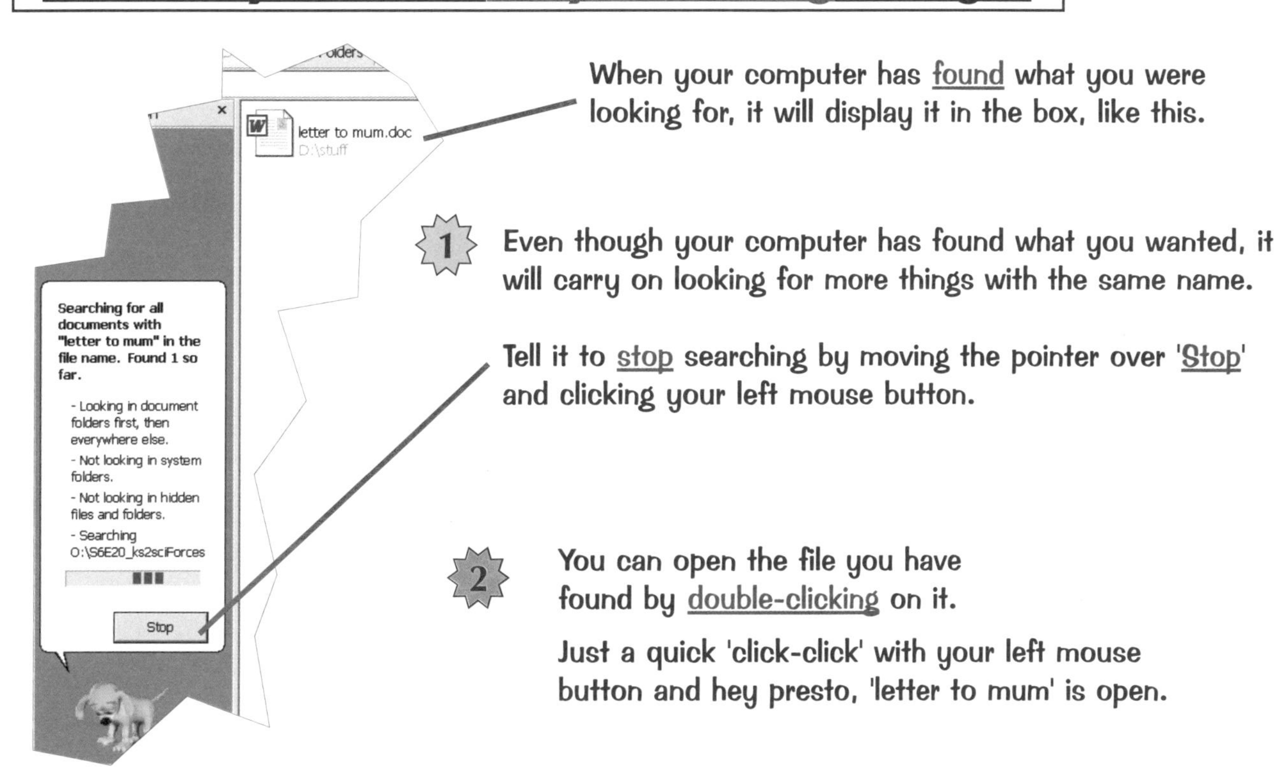

When your computer has found what you were looking for, it will display it in the box, like this.

1. Even though your computer has found what you wanted, it will carry on looking for more things with the same name.

   Tell it to stop searching by moving the pointer over 'Stop' and clicking your left mouse button.

2. You can open the file you have found by double-clicking on it.

   Just a quick 'click-click' with your left mouse button and hey presto, 'letter to mum' is open.

If you find lots of Word documents you can sort them to make finding the right one easier.

An option to 'Sort results by category' would appear. If you click on the little arrow beside it, this list of options will appear.

Clicking in the circle beside 'Name' will put all the files in alphabetical order. 'Date Modified' puts the things you've worked on recently at the top of the list.

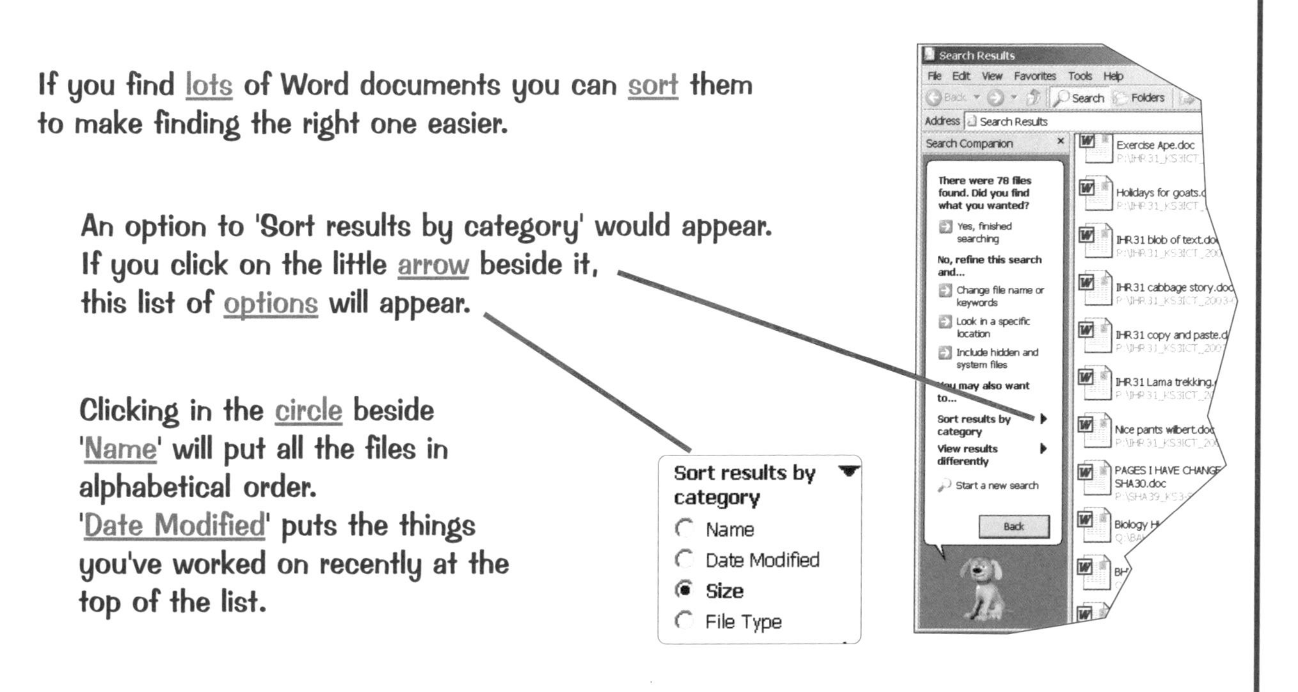

Easier than finding needles in haystacks...

Searching can be frustrating when you don't find what you're looking for straight away. However, it's just a case of being clever with what you ask your computer to look for. If you don't find it straight away, try again with other possible options, or sort your results.

Printers

You'll need to produce a paper copy of your work. You need a printer to do this.

Get to Know your Printer

Not all printers look the same, but they all have similar features.
Follow these three simple steps to get your printer ready to print:

Check the printer is switched on at the socket.

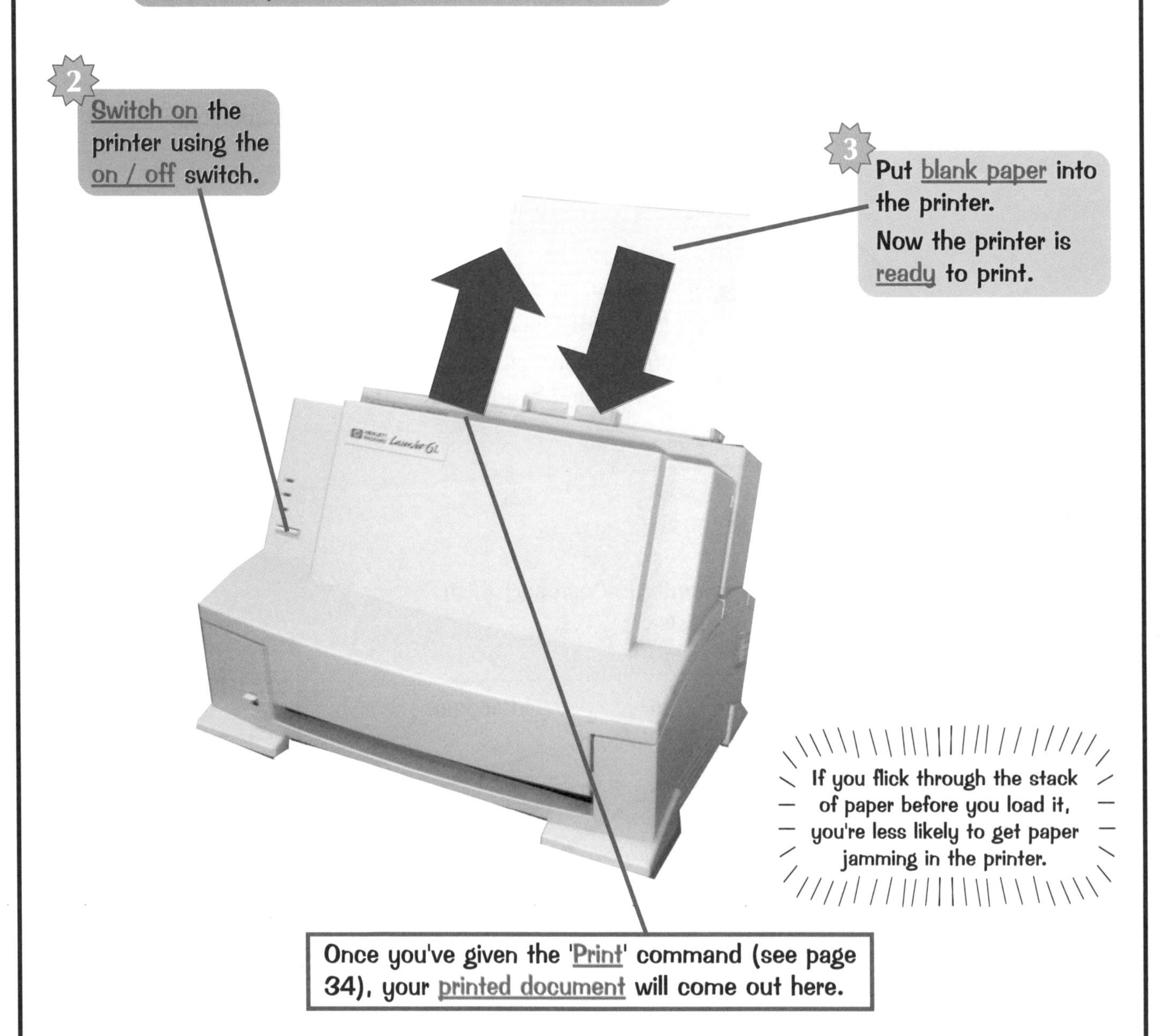

All set up and nowhere to go...

You've got the printer ready, but nothing will happen until you tell the computer to start printing. Don't panic — you'll learn how to do that later on.

Printers

There's lots of Different Kinds of Printer

All printers are slightly different, so ask your tutor to show you how to use your printer.

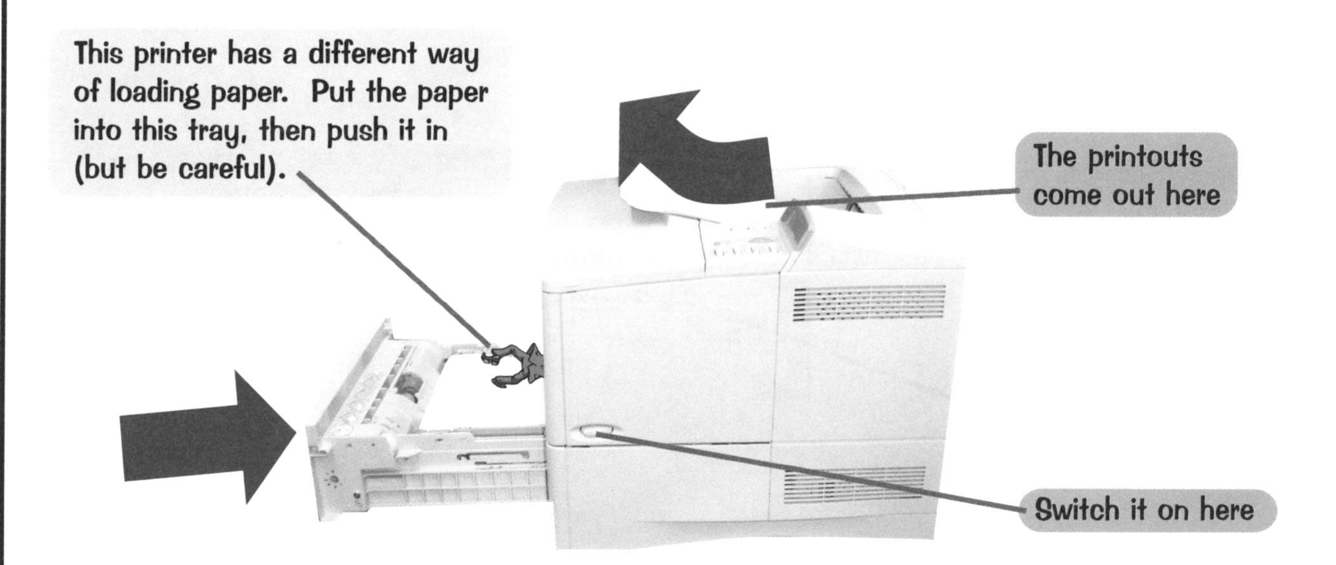

Some Printers are Designed to do Special Jobs

This is a printer designed for people who print lots of photos. It can also take bigger paper.

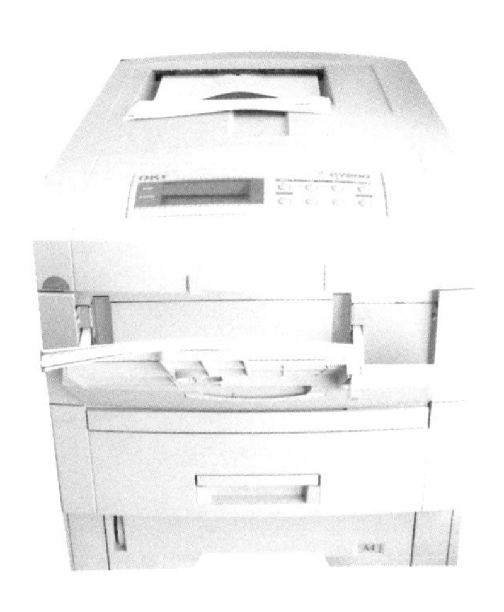

This is a colour laser printer. Laser printers make fast, high quality printouts.

Learn how to work your printer...

Get familiar with the printer you're going to use for your assessment. All you have to know is how to switch it on, where to put paper in it and where the printed paper comes out.

Printing a Document

Printing a document is pretty much the same whatever application you're using.

You can Print Documents from Most Applications

Here's how you print the Microsoft Word document 'Desserts version 1' that you created on page 29.

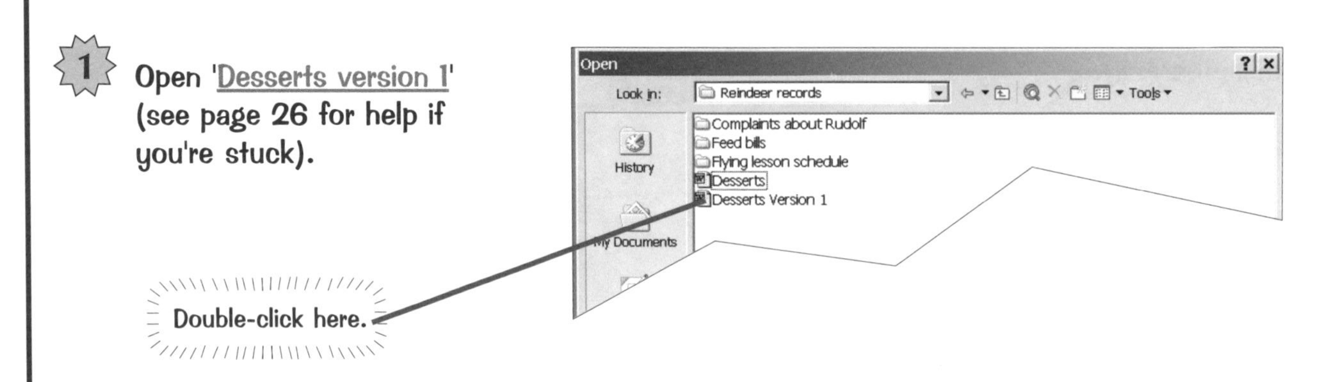

1 Open 'Desserts version 1' (see page 26 for help if you're stuck).

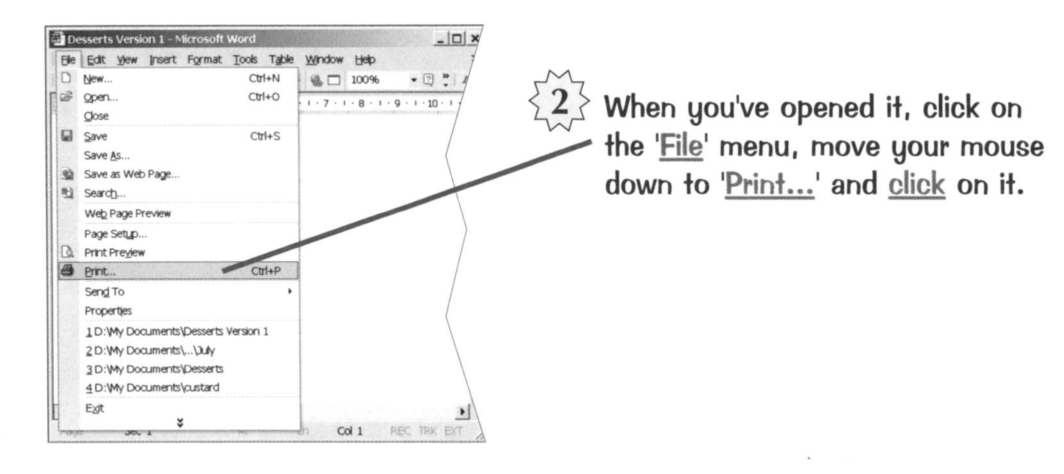

2 When you've opened it, click on the 'File' menu, move your mouse down to 'Print...' and click on it.

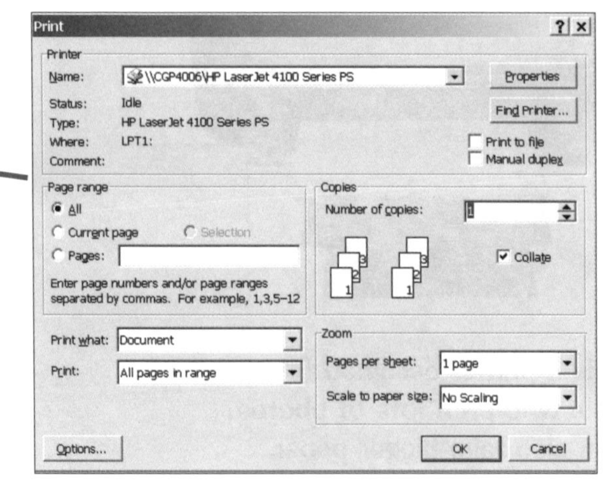

A window something like this should appear on your screen.

Print your documents to check them for errors...

It's easier to see typing mistakes on a printed copy. In the assessment, print out your documents, then check them carefully before you hand them in.

Printing a Document

You can Choose Different Printing Options

This window shows you the print options that are selected, and lets you change them.

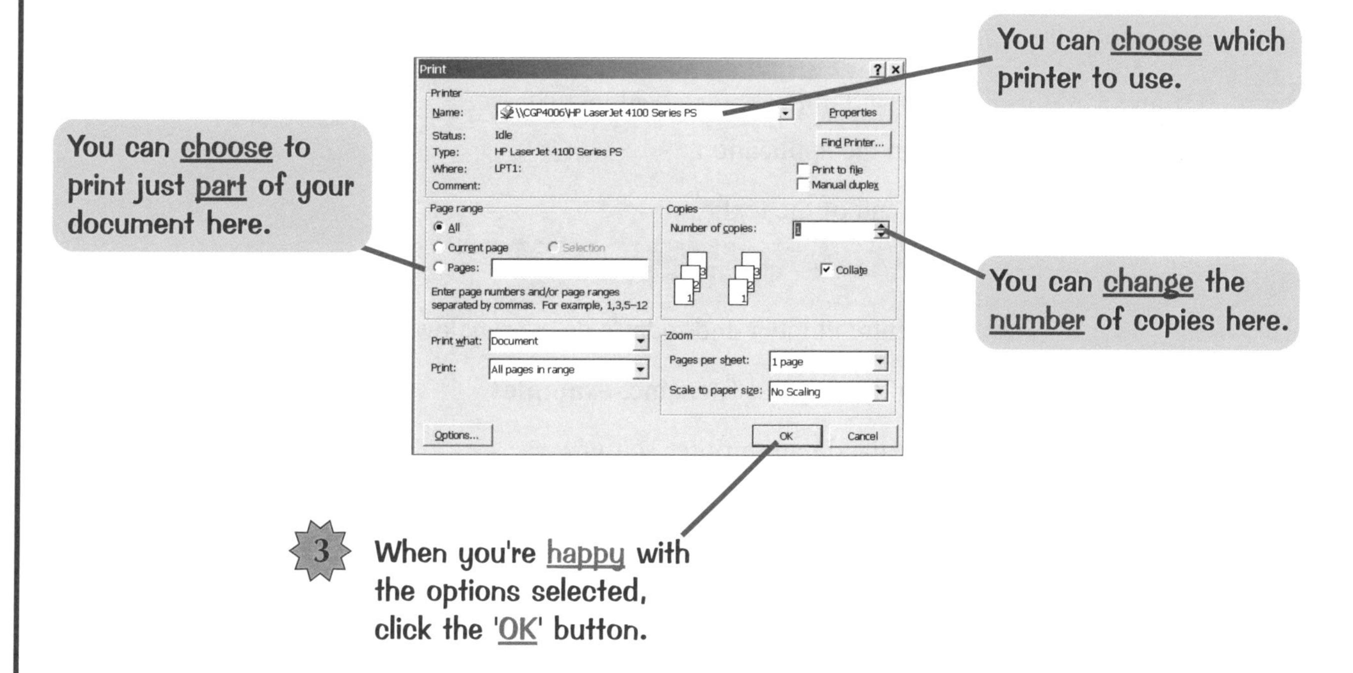

There's a Quick Way to Print Documents

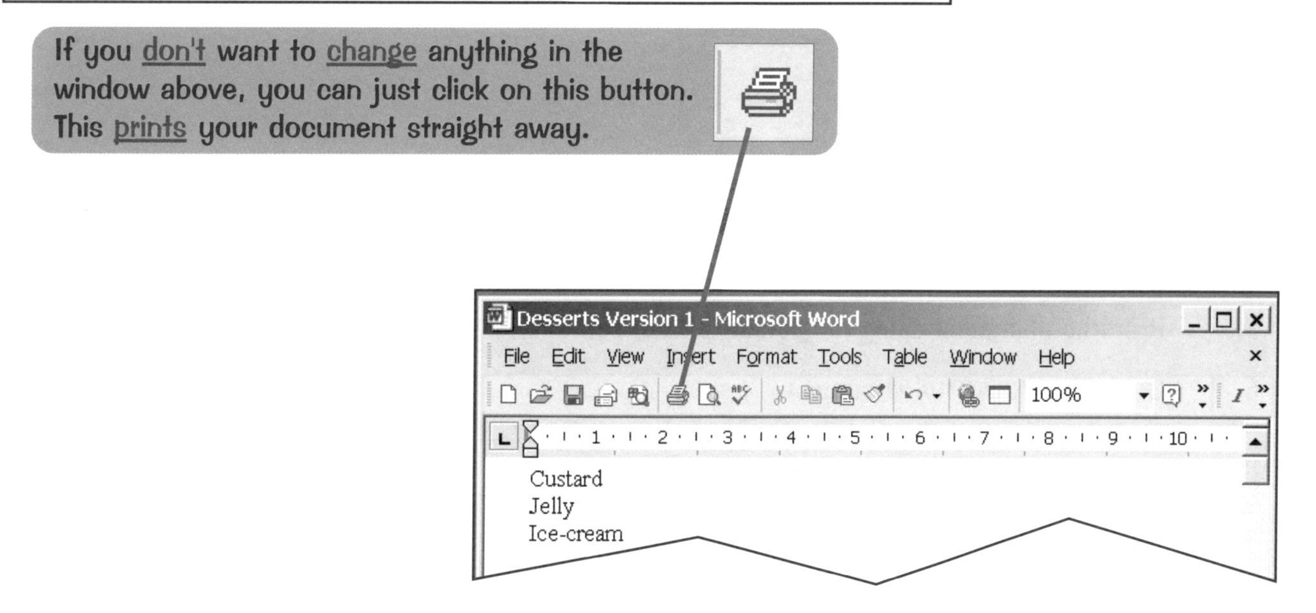

Experiment with the printing options...

Try changing the number of copies and then printing your document.
In the exam you can just use the 'default' options — the ones that are already selected.

Section Four — Practice Exercises

Practise what you've learnt so far by having a go at these exercises.

Exercise 1

1. Switch on the computer and monitor correctly and safely.
   Wait for the operating system software to load fully.
2. Using an application that will allow you to read text files,
   open the file **example1** in the application.
3. Add the following at the end of the text:

   The next meeting has been scheduled for 24/04/04.
4. Make sure your name, centre number and today's date are below the end of the text.
5. Save the document using the original filename, **example1**.
6. Print the document using the default printer settings.
7. Close the **example1** document.

Exercise 2

1. Create a new text document using a word processing application.
2. Enter the following data as shown, leaving a blank line between each line.

   Stock List Changes @ 01/04/04

   Item #234 = £2.45

   Item #789 = £6.76
3. Add your name, your centre number and today's date below the end of the text.
4. Save the document using the new filename, **stock0404**.
5. Print the document using the default printer settings.
6. Close the **stock0404** document.

Section Four — Practice Exercises

Here's some more saving and printing practice for you to try.

Exercise 3

1. Switch on the computer and monitor correctly and safely.
   Wait for the operating system software to load fully.
2. Using an application that will allow you to read text files,
   open the file **webinfo** in the application.
3. Add the following at the end of the text:

   Note Item Price (ID677#) has changed to £7.89.

4. Make sure your name, your centre number and today's date are below the end of the text.
5. Save the document using the new filename, **webinfov2**.
6. Print the document using the default printer settings.
7. Close the **webinfov2** document.

Exercise 4

1. Create a new text document using a word processing application.
2. Enter the following data as shown, leaving a space between each line.

   storage media

   floppy disks 1.44MB @ £2.49 for 10

   CD-Rewriteable disks @ £15.99 for 10

   Memory Stick 64MB @ £44.99

3. Add your name, your centre number and today's date below the end of the text.
4. Save the document using the new filename, **Storage**.
5. Print the document using the default printer settings.
6. Close the **Storage** document.

Section Four — Practice Exercises

With so many things to learn in this section we've provided two more pages of practice — lucky you eh.

Exercise 5

1. Switch on the computer and monitor correctly and safely.
   Wait for the operating system software to load fully.
2. Using the operating system's 'Find File' or 'Search' facility, find the text file **memo2**.
3. Using an application that will allow you to read text files, open the file **memo2** in the application.
4. Using the mouse and keyboard (or alternatives if available) add your name, your centre number and today's date below the end of the text.
5. Save the document using the original filename, **memo2**.
6. Print the document using the default printer settings.
7. Close the **memo2** document.

Exercise 6

1. Using the operating system's 'Find file' or 'Search' facility, find the text file **meeting04jul**.
2. Using an application that will allow you to read text files, open the file **meeting04jul** in the application.
3. Using the mouse and keyboard (or alternatives if available) add the following at the end of the text:

   Note: A number of projects will be available to view.

4. Add your name, your centre number and today's date below the end of the text.
5. Save the document using the original filename, **meeting04jul**
6. Print the document using the default printer settings.
7. Close the **meeting04jul** document.

Section Four — Practice Exercises

And yes, there's more but it's all for your own good — the more you practise now the better prepared you'll be for the assessment.

Exercise 7

1. Switch on the computer and monitor correctly and safely.
   Wait for the operating system software to load fully.
2. Using the operating system's 'Find File' or 'Search' facility, find the text file **agendaqu01**.
3. Using an application that will allow you to read text files, open the file **agendaqu01** in the application.
4. Using the mouse and keyboard (or alternatives if available) add your name, your centre number and today's date below the end of the text.
5. Save the document using the new filename, **agendaQ2**
6. Print the document using the default printer settings.
7. Close the **agendaQ2** document.

Exercise 8

1. Using the operating system's 'Find File' or 'Search' facility, find the text file **stock03**.
2. Using an application that will allow you to read text files, open the file **stock03** in the application.
3. Using the mouse and keyboard (or alternatives if available) add the following at the end of the text:

   Note: All photocopiers will be replaced at the end of the year.

4. Add your name, your centre number and today's date below the end of the text.
5. Save the document using the new filename, **stock04**
6. Print the document using the default printer settings.
7. Close the **stock04** document.

Advice for the Assessment

Once you've completed the course, you're ready to take the assessment.
These pages will give you lots of handy pieces of advice to make sure you're ready for it.

You'll get 2 Hours to Complete the Assessment

You've got plenty of time to do the assessment, so...

- Don't panic.
- Don't rush — you'll make mistakes.
- Read the instructions properly, and make sure you follow them.
- Check your work as you go along, especially your typing.
- Don't panic.

Avoid these Errors

If you make a really big error, like failing to do one of the tasks in the assessment, you won't pass, so make sure you follow the instructions carefully.

If you make more than three minor errors, you won't pass the assessment either, so avoid making small mistakes like these:

1) Making a typing (data entry) error in the data you're asked to enter. You get one error for each incorrect character / space.
2) Not typing your name, centre number and the date on your documents. (You won't lose marks if you make typing errors in this information.)

Watch Out for Data Entry Errors

When you're asked to type something, make sure you type it exactly as it's written, with the right spacing and punctuation — otherwise you're just throwing marks away. Print your documents to check for errors, then correct them on the computer before you hand them in.

Use the right case — lower case here, then use 'Shift' for upper case here.

cr0805-jtr@£2.50/K = £10

Use the 'Shift' key to get symbols like this.

Get the spacing right — there are spaces here and here.

Stay calm and you'll be fine

If you've prepared for the assessment properly, you won't have anything to worry about. You just have to show what you can do.

Advice for the Assessment

Check that you Know How to Do these Things

All you need to know to pass the assessment is in this book.
Use the checklist below to make sure you're confident with all the tasks you could be asked to do.
Go back and look at the relevant pages again if you're not sure.

	Task		Page
1)	Switch on the computer and monitor.	☐	Page 10
2)	Log on and use a password to access the computer system.	☐	Page 11
3)	Search for a file on the system.	☐	Page 30
4)	Open a file.	☐	Page 26
5)	Enter text, numbers and symbols.	☐	Page 20
6)	Change an existing document.	☐	Page 22
7)	Save an existing document.	☐	Page 29
8)	Create a new, blank document.	☐	Page 17
9)	Save a document with a new filename.	☐	Page 29
10)	Switch on the printer safely.	☐	Page 32
11)	Load paper into the printer.	☐	Page 32
12)	Print a document using the default printer settings.	☐	Page 34
13)	Close documents.	☐	Page 27
14)	Shut down the computer.	☐	Page 10

Now you're ready to do a practice test...

Once you've ticked all the boxes, you're ready for some practice assessments.
There's two over the page to get you started.

Section Five — Practice Assessment 1

Imagine this is your assessment... Take a deep breath and dive right in. You can do it.

Scenario

You are starting a new job, working as an Administrative Assistant.
You have been asked to demonstrate that you can use a computer by working through the following instructions. Your computer has been set up for you already. You have been given a password to gain access to your data. Your tutor will tell you when it will be needed.

1. Switch on the computer and monitor correctly and safely.
   Wait for the operating system software to load fully.
2. Using the operating system's 'Find File' or 'Search' facility, find the text file **agenda0407**.
3. Using an application that will allow you read text files,
   open the file **agenda0407** in the application.
4. Using the mouse and keyboard (or alternatives if available) add your name, your centre number and today's date below the end of the text.
5. Save your document using the original filename, **agenda0407**.
6. Switch on your printer and load paper.
7. Print the document using the default page settings.
8. Close the **agenda0407** document.
9. Create a new text document using the same software as you used to edit **agenda0407**.
10. Enter the following data as shown, leaving a space between each line:

    david.73@example-media

    Item: 7MG(4)=£19.65

11. Add your name, your centre number and today's date a few lines below the end of the text.
12. Save this document using the filename **info7mg**
13. Print the document using the default printer settings.
14. Close the document **info7mg**.
15. Exit the application software and shut down the operating system safely.

Section Five — Practice Assessment 2

Just in case you fancy some more assessment-style practice, here's another one.

Scenario

You are starting a new job, working as a Sales Administrator in a bicycle shop.
You have been asked to demonstrate that you can use a computer by working through the following instructions. Your computer has been set up for you already. You have been given a password to gain access to your data. Your tutor will tell you when it will be needed.

1. Switch on the computer and monitor correctly and safely.
   Wait for the operating system software to load fully.
2. Using the operating system's 'Find File' or 'Search' facility, find the text file **Invoice230**.
3. Using an application that will allow you read text files, open the file **Invoice230** in the application.
4. Using the mouse and keyboard (or alternatives if available) add your name, your centre number and today's date below the end of the text.
5. Save your document using the original filename, **Invoice230**.
6. Switch on your printer and load paper.
7. Print the document using the default page settings.
8. Close the **Invoice230** document.
9. Create a new text document using the same software as you used to edit **Invoice230**.
10. Enter the following data as shown, leaving a space between each line:

    Special Bank Holiday Promotion!

    Bikes will be available to hire at the discounted price of £11.50 an hour.

    Email: summer-hol.promotion@spokes for further details.
11. Add your name, your centre number and today's date a few lines below the end of the text.
12. Save this document using the filename **promo29b**.
13. Print the document using the default printer settings.
14. Close the document **promo29b**.
15. Exit the application software and shut down the operating system safely.

Index